EPIC

TRAINING

A COMPREHENSIVE GUIDE

TO OBSTACLE COURSE
TRAINING

RICH BORGATTI JR

Cover design by Arianne d'Entremont
Edited by Andréa Maria Cecil Topper

www.richborgatti.com
www.epicracetraining.com
www.mountainstrength.com

Print ISBN: 978-1-66783-819-9
eBook ISBN: 978-1-66783-820-5

Printed in the United States of America

EPIC

TRAINING

TESTIMONIALS

"I have worked with Rich several times, and I especially appreciated his coaching to prepare me for the 2019 World's Toughest Mudder. He crafted superb and challenging programming that helped me vastly improve my mileage and obstacle completion. As a fitness professional myself, I can say that Rich is a knowledgeable and approachable coach who provides personal support to his athletes. With his guidance, I was able to race for 24 hours, complete 50 miles, and achieve my goal of qualifying for the 2020 Obstacle Course Racing World Championship."

Jay Oppenheim, MS, CPT, CHWC

"Rich Borgatti has helped me improve my form in many exercises that I have been doing for years. This has increased my proprioception and made me less injury-prone"

Andy Boudreau, Spartan Race Elite Competitor

"When I did my first Spartan race, I failed just about every obstacle that a person can fail. Afterwards, I reached out to Rich for obstacle specific training. He helped me with both the technique and strength needed to get through the obstacles, and as a result, I ended up on some podiums!"

Caroline Staudt, Spartan Race Ultra Athlete

"Coach Rich helped me train for my first Spartan Race and then my first 14.86 mile race up the mountains of Aspen. He gave me a plan that I was able to execute against to finish my race feeling strong!"

Carolyn Kim, Half Marathon Athlete

"I've worked with Rich for years and he's a terrific coach. Rich has taught me a ton over the years, but one huge highlight is that he taught me how to throw a spear, and how to do it more than just once! Since learning the proper technique from Rich, I've made almost all my spear throws, including both at the 2019 Killington Ultra, one of which was in the dark!"

David Fatula, OCR Athlete

TABLE OF CONTENTS

ACKNOWLEDGEMENTS

I would like to start off by thanking my wonderful wife, Arianne. Without you there is so much I would not have accomplished. You truly made sacrifices and cleared so many obstacles from the path for me to be able to author this book. You contributed to this book in so many ways, from the cover to listening to my roadblocks. You rescheduled our life to give me space to write, wrangled the kids out of the office and encouraged me to keep going when it got tough. Without your support and encouragement my life would be full of high school war stories and not of accomplishments. I love you and thank you deeply.

To my sons, I do all these things so one day when you dream of doing something grand, I can say and mean it when I tell you that you can do anything. I hope one day to be able to watch you do what others call impossible.

To Mom and Dad, you gave me all I needed in life and more. You always let me be myself and encouraged me to do all I wanted to do. Thank you for all the support, calls, driving to sports practices and games, and above all the lessons on being a good person.

Over the many years I have had quite a few involved mentors in my life, of which I am extremely grateful for their guidance and encouragement.

To Frank Massaro, my Scoutmaster of Troop 18 Revere, you saw something in this little city kid, you guided me to leadership and the outdoors. You cared at a time I thought I was alone, outcast, and quite lost. You did more for me than I was able to articulate in my teenage mind. Lessons that took years to bloom. You showed me that I could be a leader. Thank you for helping lay the foundation of leadership skills that I now have.

To Mark Davis, My martial arts teacher, friend, guide and first business mentor. You have never ceased to amaze me with your lessons, wisdom and caring. You helped me forge my body and mind together. You gave me tests of character and encouraged me after every fall. All the while showing me that a smile and strength of character are stronger than any martial technique. My confidence was built through your guidance and Dojo, The Boston Martial Arts Center. Thank you for being such a strong example of what I could be.

To Chris Cooper, you inspired me from afar at first with your blog posts. When I reached the hardest moments in my business you answered the call. You saved my dream. My family and I thank you. You encouraged me when I wanted to go all in on OCR training as a coach and gave me a platform to bring it to others. You lifted me up and gave my passion light and helped me grow as a coach and business owner. You gave me permission to reach farther and do so with a helping hand.

To Jeff Godin and Joe DiStefano, thank you both for creating the Spartan SGX coaches' course. This Coaching Certification was needed for our racing community and you both made something amazing. It truly set a high bar for standards as coaches in a complex and evolving industry. Thank you for the years of friendship and trust. You allowed me to better myself as well as others. I am so proud to have collaborated with you both and the community of coaches that you brought together.

To TJ Murphy, you saved this book. You may not have known it at the time when you walked through the doors at my gym, but you did. Your advice and confidence in this project made me jump back in full force. It was overwhelming and I was at a loss on how to continue. Thank you for encouraging me, reading early drafts, and allowing me to expand my writing to the Spartan website. Every time I wrote a blog post it opened another piece of inspiration for this book. Without our meeting this project may have never seen the light of day. Thank you.

To all my mentors and guides in the Two Brain Business family, Chris Cooper, Josh Price, Peter Brasovan, I owe you all a big hug, high five and a cup of coffee. To my Editors, Mike Warkentin and Andrea Maria Cecil Topper, thank you so much.

To Josh, your calm and reassuring voice and guidance was most needed juggling multiple projects and businesses. Thank you for cutting through the noise and saying, "Do This".

To Peter, thank you for helping keep me on track mentoring me and my business during a pandemic and then back on track to publish this book.

To Mike, your confidence that this could be a good book was what I needed to hear. Thank you for taking this project on and getting the right people in the right seats.

To, Andrea, you took my mess of writing and made it look like a book. Who knew I needed chapters? You organized and restructured such a mess that I am impressed at what we turned it into. Thank you for all the phone calls, editing and lessons on writing and focus.

To everyone past and present that has ever been involved in the Mountain Strength CrossFit community and gym. Thank you for trusting me with your fitness and adding to the amazing community that we have.

To Paul Bernardi and John Mariani, thank you for training and racing all those early OCRs with me. It meant the world to me to be at the start line with you. To all my coaches past and present, thank you for being part of the team and changing lives through fitness.

To my private OCR athletes, much of this book came from what I needed to learn to support you in your racing seasons. You brought enthusiasm and passion for OCR to every workout and race. I am truly one lucky coach to have collaborated with you all. Keep the fire alive and race on!

Brandon Stumpf, Alex Wisch, Caroline Straudt, Danielle and Mike Fenton Rosevalley, Dave and Ami Fatula, Mike Downey, Josh Fiore, Jay Oppenheim, Justin Moss, Nele Schulze, Paul Jones and the scores of NE Spahtens and all athletes online that answered my call to test out the workouts in this book. Thank you all!

Thank you, Brooke Bass and Dave Fatula, for taking time out of your day to get the pictures into the book. Your "let's get it done" attitude really helped speed those photo sessions along. Much appreciated.

Thank you to everyone that has attended my OCR classes, workshops, and seminars over the past 10 years. It has been an enlightening ride and I hope for more to come.

Thank you so much to all who helped back this book on Kickstarter. We would not have been able to publish this book without your help.

Margaret Hoffman

Linda Borgatti

Diane and Ed Boggs

Dorothy McCuen

Walter "JR" Kuketz

Tony Fanara

Sara Fleming

Robb Ellis

The Creative Fund by BackerKit

Theodore E. Jeveli

Jasper Walters

Brooke Bass

David Fatula

Mike LeJeune

Brian Vernaglia

M L

Andrea Savard

Le Grand Reynolds

Troy Midkiff

Brad Cox

William Band

Dylan Reach

Joe Pagliuca

Joseph Crehan

Anthony Passamonte

Matthew Fanara

Chris Cooper

Emanuel Pacheco

Stratton Newbert

Eric Jeveli

Laura Wolfinger

CM Frampton

Jahx

Jim Heffernan

Shannon Davis

Marco Caromba

Ben Gould

Dawn P.

Chris Couture

Rebecca Winter

Kevin Cafferty

Mike Flanagan

Sarah Adelmann

Christine Ouellette

Angela Froio Doyle

Marie Simpson

Lisa Ouellette

Bill Brickman

Karen

Kel

Jeff Godin

Peter B.

George Kalos

Joshua J Grenell

Gary Lombardo

Chris Canfield

Todd Cambio

Jay Oppenheim

Sean M.

Charlene Band

Kristen Webb

Sean McDermott

Christopher Tretter

Sarah Visinski

Balazs Szemes

Arianne d'Entremont Borgatti

Lyska BE

Rob Walsh

Dave McManus

Terri Feldman

Ron Fuller

Robert Doyle

Sally Robinson

Gena Bronson

Mark Andersen

Leanne Marrama

Rachel Miller

John C. Mariani

Jay Celat

Warren

Jasmine

Joseph B Towers

Covering New England

Brandon Stumpf

Paul Bernardi

Justin Keane

Danielle Rosvally

Nanci Johnson

Mike Deibler

Alex Wisch

David Meyer

Nancy Krouse

Katie and Matt Fanara

Max "JJ"

FOREWORD

I met Coach Borgatti for the first time at his facility in October of 2013 when he hosted a Spartan SGX workshop. Coach was a welcoming, generous, and gracious host. We immediately made a connection because of a shared philosophy of life, coaching, and training practices. Since that time Rich has been a strong supporter of Spartan, Spartan SGX, and the sport of OCR. Every time I race in New England, we seem to find each other out on the course.

Coach Borgatti attended our first SGX Level 2 coach certification in Boston. The workshop had two days of lecture and discussion followed by the third day that included travel to the birthplace of Spartan, Pittsfield, VT, where candidates went through a grueling day of Spartan Death Race like activities. Aside from his Spartan SGX credentials he has earned numerous credentials in the area of endurance racing and natural movement to strengthen his knowledge base. Despite his level of expertise, he is always seeking new knowledge and finding ways to improve his coaching and training methods. His work has been so impressive, Spartan honored him in 2019 as one of the top 10 Coaches.

When I saw Coach was authoring a book, I nodded to myself and thought he is the perfect person for this work. Rich had been racing OCR since before I met him. He has trained thousands of clients for the sport OCR. His experience, knowledge, and drive make him a bonified expert in this space.

It was with great interest that I had the opportunity to read the pre-release edition of Coach Borgatti's book. Training for the sport of OCR is no easy task. It is complex and multidimensional. To perform well in the sport of OCR an athlete needs to be strong, have a high aerobic capacity, move well, and have a high anaerobic capacity. The book you are about to read includes evidence-based practices to improve fitness in all the dimensions of fitness important to the sport of OCR and in life in general. This book is appropriate for novice and elite athletes alike. I would also encourage anyone interested in general fitness to read this book because OCR training is the highest form of functional fitness.

Coach Borgatti covers important topics such as racing gear, running technique, and racing strategies. Coach's section on Obstacle Specific Training dives deep into obstacle technique and provides a real-life perspective on how to complete the obstacles. The reader will find the balance between science and practical application to be refreshing. Enough science to understand the why and plenty of real-life how so the reader can act today.

I am honored that Coach Borgatti asked me to write this forward. I have deep respect not only for his coaching and training methods but his human spirit as well. This book is a testament to his life's work in this area and it shines brightly.

Jeff Godin, Ph.D.

Professor, Head of Performance and Sport Science,

Dept. Exercise and Sport Science, Fitchburg State University

Head of Fitness Education, Spartan Race

PREFACE

With this book, I hope to bring the world of Obstacle Course Racing (OCR) to more people. And let them know that "Yes, you too, can do these crazy races!" This book is meant to help remove any hesitation or fear of trying an obstacle course race, also called OCR for short. To give proper training advice and an insight into the many layers, distances and people who have conquered an OCR. Many people look at the race from the outside and see the things that they cannot do or are afraid of, such as climbing a rope. With good instruction and guidance these obstacles can conquered.

This book is meant to help athletes that have become bored with the same old running and fitness routine and may want something different. Something with more than one dimension to it. Obstacle Course Racing has many facets and I hope I can help transition a single sport athlete into this growing hybrid athlete sport.

Throughout the book I will have sections for trainers and coaches. In these sections I will talk about my perspective as a coach and give advice and guidance on teaching the information to athletes from a coach's perspective.

This book does not have to be read front to back. Instead, it is set up in a way that will allow you to jump around chapters if needed. If you are reading this close to a race you may want to jump straight to the obstacle section to learn a few tips and tricks before the race. If your race is three to four months away and can work on strength work as well as running form you can jump right to the training and running sections. Please use this book the best way for your racing season.

This book is for everyone who wants to run a healthy race, maybe compete in their age group, but mostly the newer athletes and the coaches that want to teach anyone to get involved with obstacle course racing. These races can change your life. This book is meant to alleviate fear and doubt and give you a plan to conquer a physical and mental challenge, to give you access to something that can be a catalyst of change for you. To awaken something that may be lying deep within, dormant but primal, necessary but hidden. It's a push and a guide into the unknown.

What This Book Is Not

This book is not necessarily for the super athlete, the 1% elites, although they may gain a trick or two as they read. While I do occasionally train pro OCR athletes, mostly my work has been with training regular people trying their first race. In this book we will only be covering the basics and the beginning stages of an OCR athlete in general terms. This book will not delve too deep into exercise science or nutrition. If you need more advanced information or help, send an email to rich@epicracetraining.com

INTRODUCTION

I got to the mountain a bit late, after a 4-hour car ride I jogged from the car to the start line. I was rushed, but calm. I did not yet realize how unprepared I was. That would come after 2 hours on the mountain when my calves started to cramp, I realized that I did not have enough food or water. We ended up being on that mountain for 6 hours and I only had enough food and water for 3. At the 3 hour mark my body also realized this and my hamstrings and quads locked up, I could only move up hill in short bursts before the pain was too much and then I started crawling.

"I think I am going to die here…"

I thought, lying in the dirt on the side of a mountain in Vermont on May 2nd, 2012. The sky looked peaceful in contrast to the throngs of people marching up the mountain past me. They were dirty, bloody, bruised but determined. They marched on while I lay there, staring at the sky. A few nice enough to ask, inquired if I was okay, I waved them on not wanting to admit defeat aloud. I needed to rest and think.

How did I get here? How did I arrive at this point where my body refused to work, and cramps wracked my body? My lungs burning and my self-doubt loud and clear. I had laid down and not even told my teammates

I had run out of steam. I let them keep running ahead. My question haunted me. My expectations and reality had clearly gone in separate directions. What should I do? Walk off the mountain or continue?

After my moment of reflection, I felt that I had rested enough and was determined to get back up on my feet and continue. It was then when I saw a hand reach down to me. My teammates, Paul and Jeff, had returned. "We all finish together," they said. And there it was, the moment that made me smile again and see the magic in these races. Teamwork and shared suffering. We were all going through the same challenge and here to help each other, in a race as well as in life. We can all get through it if we go together. I got up on my feet and felt renewed. We shuffled off together to finish the last few miles and obstacles together.

Before this moment, in 2010, an athlete I was training named Mike W. asked me to write him a program for this new challenge he signed up for called a "Tough Mudder". There was not much info on it as it was new. It seemed intriguing and challenging. It was ten miles on a mountain with crazy obstacles they were trying to keep a secret. I had an endurance, climbing and hiking background so I developed a program from what little I knew about a "Tough Mudder" and their website description.

Mike did great and had no issues. He said he was the only one on his team that was prepared for the arduous hikes and crazy obstacles. Slowly more clients started getting interested and doing the Warrior Dash (now defunct) and Spartan Races. They had a blast, and we had a great training program for the athletes that did the races. This was the beginning of Obstacle Course Racing; the wild west of mud runs. Most races in the beginning tried to stay mysterious so you did not know what you were in for. Races routinely advertised that they were a 5K only to turn out to be a 5M! It was exciting and you never knew what challenge would face you on the course.

I was in the middle of expanding my gym and awaiting our first child to arrive in 2011. After my son was born and the gym was opened, I signed up for my first Tough Mudder challenge. 10+ miles, up and down a mountain. Over and through multiple challenging obstacles. By now there were lots of videos and write ups on these races. I thought I would be fine for the challenge, even a bit too confident in hindsight. In review I neglected serious time on my feet and not enough elevation training. With a newborn child I was lacking sleep and proper nutrition which also led to under recovery from the CrossFit workouts I was doing. I wrote a great program for my clients, but I failed to stick to my own advice and program. In a sense I ended up being my own worst client.

If only I had some salt or other electrolytes! My teammates Paul and Jeff were doing fine, they followed the program I outlined and were prepared. They kept me in great spirits and stayed alongside me or waited for me at checkpoints. At some point I just felt like I was holding them back, so I stopped. And now we are back at my moment of reflection as I lay on my back. It would have been easy to completely give in and walk off the course. To give in to the pain and embarrassment I felt. I mean, I was in shape... wasn't I? I started to see all the mistakes I had made, the short cuts and the ways I was unprepared. I vowed then to fix it all. To deconstruct my experience and build it all back up. To make this pain worth it and help others so they didn't have to make these same mistakes.

I often look back at my finisher photos of this race. You can see the pain and the grimace as I cross the finish line. But what they do not show is the pride I had in myself for getting back up, the trust and support I felt from my teammates, and the changes that were made inside me that day.

This book is the culmination of that vow I made to myself on the side of that mountain. My pledge to help others and pass on my knowledge and mistakes. To share the pain but to also give you, the reader, hope. Hope that when it gets tough, and you are experiencing the suffer fest that is an Obstacle Course Race, that you too can get back up and keep going. Since this race I have been back to Tough Mudder 3 more times, Warrior Dash, and more than 20 Spartan races from Stadions to Beasts.

I am certified through Spartan Race's SGX coaching Level 2 and Obstacle Course Specialist Programs. I have immersed myself in the culture, training and community of OCR and have developed a tribe of my own and have been involved in training thousands of athletes since 2010. From my own athletes in the gym at Mountain Strength CrossFit and online with Epic Race Training to huge 1 day Spartan World Tour training events with hundreds (and in one case one thousand people) attending. It is possible to train and finish these races and their challenges and I can show you how to cross that finish line.

1

A VERY SHORT HISTORY OF OCR

Photo: R. Borgatti

Obstacle Course Races really came into the mainstream in 2010 with Tough Mudder, Spartan Race, and Warrior Dash holding their inaugural public events. Before these races there were military style obstacle courses, adventure races, eco races, and the Death Race (Peak Races Pre-Spartan). But the widely accessible, community oriented and diverse races we now see were bred from the first events that Spartan and Tough Mudder started in 2010.

These races in the last decade have developed into multi-tier distances, multiple laps, time trials, World Championships and Olympic bids. In the early days of OCR, you had to travel to remote areas and ski parks to race. Now the sport has grown so much that you can view the races on TV and the internet.

There are also races in urban environments like sports stadiums. Most major races are now within a 4-hour drive of every major city. The obstacles that were once crafted from homemade materials like logs and 2x4s that all had a natural but low budget feel to them. The obstacles are now aluminum and steel with tall structures and need cranes and backhoes to help create the courses. The course equipment is now trucked across the country like a concert stage, courses can now get set up quicker and hold greater challenges than ever before. These once backyard races have now evolved to big time entertainment venues.

As these races go from small endurance challenges to big racing events there will be changes. Some of the early pioneer races have closed or have been absorbed (Ex: Spartan Race now owns Warrior Dash and Tough Mudder - 2020). Some, like Tough Mudder have had to weather serious legal battles and leadership changes over the years. As these races pass the 10-year mark and move from infancy to maturity, we should expect to see even more changes.

Local races and communities, like the New England Spahtans group in the Northeast and their #Racelocal series have formed a grassroots movement over the years to support the growing interest in the sport and to foster a welcoming environment.

Communities like theirs help small local race series get started and get people involved. Finding a local community to be a part of is highly recommended, whether it is in a gym environment or with an online community. It is important to help support small local races as well as the big global companies. Both have their place in keeping the scene vibrant, engaging, challenging and innovative. For a great example of this check out the F.I.T. Challenge series (http://www.fitchallenge.org/)

Do your best to support local companies, programs, coaches, gyms and events in your area. They are the glue that holds it all together and puts a soul into the scene. Even the big companies started off as a crazy idea in the woods.

2

THE WHY AND WHO
OF OBSTACLE COURSE RACING

Photo: H. Marte, Spartan Media, HubSpot Boston Spartan team

Why Should I Run an Obstacle Course Race?

Mud, water, obstacles, and running through the woods? Why is it that these races and challenges have been gaining in popularity since 2010? Why are people paying money to suffer and get dirty? To hang on bars and crawl under wire? What are they getting out of it and is it something that you could too? There is even a documentary about these races and the people ("Rise of the Sufferfests"). Is it that they have always loved running in the mud? Perhaps, but my experience talking with fellow racers on the mountains and at community gatherings tells a story of a desire to challenge themselves and to answer a burning question "Can I do that?".

These races, mud runs, and physical challenges usually represent a steppingstone to a larger goal in life. A physical challenge that they are undertaking as a catalyst to some sort of change. It can sometimes be a mental or physical change, or just a sense of accomplishment and confidence. For many it's a big enough goal that they will work hard to achieve the results they desire.

I have met people who could not run a mile without stopping or walking and then they sign up for a 3-mile Spartan Sprint race. The commitment to a goal helped them get out of bed every morning for months and get on the road to run, to find a trainer to teach them how to climb a rope, to further their knowledge and skill set. *To be a different person after the race than when they started.*

This is what it was like for me during my first 14 Mile Spartan Beast race at Killington Mountain in Vermont. Completing the course made me feel like a different person. I felt like I was stripped bare and rebuilt by the end of that Spartan Beast. I remember feeling all the things I thought were problems or hardships before the race melted away and were replaced with gratitude for what I had. I was lucky to be there, to be alive and experience life at a different volume and tempo. This is not entirely a unique experience I found out. I was not alone in feeling this transformation as many other racers have also felt a life changing or perspective altering experience at these races. Why and how does this happen? I offer an inside look to some of the reasons here and throughout the book.

An Obstacle race has many physical challenges and benefits such as gaining stamina, endurance, and strength of the mind, body and in some cases the spirit. It can tax your mind and spirit while pushing you towards completing tasks that you never thought possible.

Some of my greatest moments as an OCR coach have been watching people climb over 6' and 8' walls or up a 15' rope when before preparing for a race they never thought they would ever be able to do it. Many of us may hold onto a horrible memory of gym class PE tests or the President's physical challenge where you had to climb a very tall rope in elementary school, a task which many failed at. These races are a chance to erase those negative memories of failed physical challenges and push through to write a new story for ourselves about what we ARE and can be capable of. A new version of ourselves.

We can conquer the mental and physical feats and create space for adventure in our lives. We can go and do crazy things with our friends like race over a mountain and drag tires through the woods and scale a 15' rope into the air and ring a bell and say, "I AM ALIVE!" and prove to ourselves we are not wasting away in a cubicle or an office. We are something much more and full of adventure.

Obstacle racing is growing along a similar trajectory as the Triathlon scene has in the last 30 years. A truly mixed modal endurance sport that requires some training but not the level of dedication as an Ironman event. A triathlon consists of 3 consecutive events (swim, bike, run). These movements all live in the frontal plane of the body, moving in the same direction.

The new mixed modal, or hybrid athlete, needs strength in multiple planes and directions to lift, pull, push and carry. Stamina and endurance for running and carrying heavy loads long distances. Explosiveness to flip a tire, jump high, throw a spear. Flexibility and range of motion to swing and climb over and through obstacles.

The new mixed modal races express the full being of a hybrid athlete and move the athlete in many directions, we twist, pull, push, run, jump, climb, crawl, go forward, backwards and sideways until we reach the finish line.

Who Does an Obstacle Course Race?

Photo: Spartan Media, Athletes:
A. Fatula, D. Fatula, R. Borgatti, H. Cooke

What kind of people do obstacle course racing?

The kind that are supportive and looking for a challenge. I have seriously not met a mean or unhelpful person in this sport yet. Out on the course or in training we all know that we are in some way challenging ourselves. The races can be intimidating even to just sign up for one. So if you made it to the start line you had to look a bit inside yourself to get there, and if you finished the race we all know what you went through, to a degree, to get there and we can bond over the shared suffering and challenges.

One misconception I hear all the time from people who have not done one is that you need to be a runner to participate in an obstacle race. This is just not true. You can hike or walk almost every race that I have attended. You will be done faster if you run, but it is never a requirement. You just need to finish before the end of the day or a specified cut off time. I have been on the course with multiple racers that were blind, missing limbs, and over 70 yrs. old! I was often humbled and inspired to be on the same course as these racers. It just shows the accessibility of these challenges and the character of the people they attract. The old adage of "If you have a will, there's a way" holds true in this arena.

Are They Crazy??

You may be asking yourself "Why do people pay money and spend their time getting dirty and putting themselves through this suffer fest?" What is it that got them started? How did they train? Were they already super athletes just looking for the next challenge? Or ordinary everyday people, with a job and family?

A common response after explaining what an Obstacle Course Race is would be, "Oh I could never do that!". This is understandable as a race can have many challenges to the novice. Anyone can do these races and overcome the challenges. In the appendix are interviews with some of my past clients and fellow racers to find out what made them do these races. Where did they start and how far have, they gone? Was this just a one-time occurrence or did it change them and put them on a new path?

Read the Athlete Interviews and training stories in the Appendix at the end of the book. These stories cover the spectrum of beginner to elite, and weekend hobbyist racer. You will see that not everyone starts off in crazy good shape or already an elite athlete. Perhaps you too will find inspiration in their stories as I did and go for a goal outside of your comfort zone.

3

GETTING STARTED

Photo: Spartan Media Team, Athletes:
P. Bernardi, J. Mariani, R. Borgatti

Get moving! The biggest thing you can do is acclimate to the distance of the race. If you signed up for a 5k race, then you need to be able to travel that far. Start by walking, then jogging. See how far you can go in 20 mins, then 30, then 45 mins. Can you make it 5k walking? How long did it take you? Then walk/jog and finally get to jog the whole distance. Acclimating to the distance should take roughly 4-6 weeks of 2-3x week cardio sessions incrementing the distance each week. Check out the beginner run program later in the book.

What about the obstacles? This will depend on your athletic background and current fitness level. If you are just getting off the couch after a large period of inactivity it would be best to find a knowledgeable fitness or OCR coach in the area as well as get cleared by a physician for activity.

Most obstacles will require you to be able to carry, move and hang onto something. This means that you will need to be able to be strong enough to push, pull and support your own body weight. Get started by hiking and carrying objects. Then work on moving your body over and under objects like low walls or park benches. You don't need to be fast, just moving forward.

Choosing a First Race

Truth be told, I do not know many people who chose their first race on their own. Most people that start Obstacle Course Races are dragged through the mud by a best friend or training buddy. Most of my OCR athletes started off in my CrossFit gym and saw a group of us training for a race and wanted in on the crazy looking, fun things we were doing. Crazy endeavors are always best to do as a group. So, the short answer to how to "Choose Your First Race" is to find a friend, gym or social group (such as work, church, runners, intramural, online) and join them for a race.

My advice to first time racers is go short first. It doesn't matter if you are a first-time athlete or an elite runner, triathlete, space fighter pilot, etc. go for a short race first. It will be more fun, and you won't feel too much pressure to over perform. Do not hold yourself to any expectations in regard to placement, finishing time etc. I like first time racers to just have the expectation of experiencing the obstacles and challenges themselves wherever they are at. It is also easy on the wallet and often easier to train for.

The Spartan Stadium series or similar urban race is best to start with for non-runners or those that don't like to run too much. These races are 2-3M in distance but pack as many obstacles in them as a 5M race. These distance races are perfect to do with lots of friends. There is no mud and plenty of places to eat and hang out nearby. Also great for little racers like kids and teens as well to start getting involved in OCR. Many have a short course for small kids (.5M) and a longer course for teens (1M)

Bonus: You do not need to go to the bathroom in the woods! There are often lots of clean bathroom spots along the course.

If you are coming into this sport with a strong endurance/trail running background the 5k or 10k series would be the best to start off with. In the Spartan Races these would be a Sprint or a Super.

Although, I have known a handful of people who started with a Half Marathon distance race (Spartan Beast) or a 10M Tough Mudder. Be aware that the terrain is a lot more challenging on these longer races/challenges. Having some experience running a Half Marathon distance race will be very helpful here. My half marathon road race time is 2 hours but my first Half Marathon Beast on Killington Mountain in Vermont took me 8 hours to complete.

Considerations when choosing a race

Whether it is your first or 100th race, planning for the race will need to be done. Here I will lay out some considerations that will help make the planning process easier. While this is by no means an exhaustive list it should serve to remove some blind spots when choosing and planning for a race or multiple races in a season.

How much time for training do you have?

The longer the race distance the more training time you will need to ramp up. Some suggested minimum training times needed for each distance; I include longer races in here as a comparison:

- 5K: 4-6 weeks
- 10K: 6 weeks
- 10M: 6-8 weeks
- 14M: 8-12 weeks
- Ultra: 12-16 weeks

Do you have a training buddy or team?

Having someone to workout with and train for a race will greatly increase your chances of getting to the starting line. Lack of goal setting and accountability are the main reasons athletes skip workouts and give up. If you cannot find a training partner you will be able to find a team at a local gym or check for an online community that you can meet up with or at least help keep you accountable to your training and goals. If you tell someone a goal you are more likely to accomplish it. So, grab a friend or two to train with.

What should I wear?

Obstacle Course races are known for strange weather and varying terrain. Refer to the OCR Gear section to get an in-depth list of what to wear. The basic list would be:

- Running shorts or tights
- Technical shirt (Non cotton)
- Sports Bra (Women)
- Non cotton underwear (Men/Women)
- Long socks
- Trail running sneakers

Will you be running in the dark?

If your start time is late, you may be running in the dark. Make sure you know the time of sunrise and sunset for racing day if you have an early or late start. You will need a headlamp and possibly glow sticks if you are on a mountain but will not for a stadium race (They have lights!).

I always suggest having a glow stick and headlamp in your bag regardless of start time or estimated finish. This is also great to have for training. Not everyone's schedule will line up so that we can do training runs in the light. You may need to run outside in the early morning or late at night. If you are running on the road in the dark, wear a safety reflective vest.

Will there be water obstacles?

Most Obstacle Races will have a water element to them. These water obstacles may be a quick dunk, a lengthy wade or a full immersion swim. If so you may need clothing that dries quickly or water proof secured clothing to put on should hyperthermia sets in. Some longer races (such as World's Toughest Mudder) require a wetsuit. Most beginners will not need to worry about water training. The best training for these obstacles is to train wet so don't avoid the rain on run days. Get comfortable being wet.

Will there be a change in the weather?

Being aware of the weather is crucial if you are racing in the mountains. The weather and temperature can be vastly different at the top of a mountain versus the bottom. This is evident in the weather changes during the late fall races in the Northeast and the high elevation races in places like Utah.

Will I need food?

For races that are 10k in distance or have lots of elevation I suggest some supplementation in the form of calories and sugars like bars, goo's, or gels. This will become apparent during training when and how much you will need. If you estimate that you will be on the course for 2+ hours you will need to eat at the 1-hour mark. This could be a hard 5K course that you are walking/hiking or a half marathon that you are moving fast.

Have your in-race supplementation packed in your hydration pack or belt in a way that is easy to get to. If you are running with a teammate, show them where your supplements are before the race in case, they need to get it for you.

Race Day and Travel

It is a great idea to get to the race venue early enough to go through parking, meet up with teammates, check your bags and go to the bathroom. If you want to eat before the race starts, do so at least 45 mins before the start time and nothing but fluids after that. Try to use the bathroom again 20 mins before the start.

If the race venue is more than 3hrs away by car, consider going up the night before and staying at a hotel that is close by. Sitting in a car for 2+ hours and then trying to run will be challenging. You want to give yourself enough time before the race to warm up and limber up. That means about 15-20 mins of light jogging and dynamic stretches and movements. Do your best to not just get out of the car or hotel and walk up to the start line. Plan time to warm up.

4

OCR GEAR - WHAT TO WEAR

Photo: R. Borgatti

The most popular question a new racer often asks is what gear to get. What hydration pack do I need? What shoes? What do I wear at the race?

Every online group or forum is littered almost daily with these questions. Luckily these days companies are creating good products around this niche sport of OCR. You can find lots of OCR shoes on the market and OCR clothes and packs. But choosing the right one for you or the specific race you are running can be challenging.

A new racer just needs basic gear to get them to the finish line or through your first season. After that it is a good idea to invest in better gear if you will continue. My current sneakers have lasted 3 seasons, also my pack (this is my third) has lasted 5 years. Good stuff will last even if you are running it literally through the mud and rocks.

Footwear

What is the terrain? This is an important question because it determines the type of shoe you need to wear at the race. Many a first-time racer has shown up wearing basketball shoes or running shoes that have no grip or edges to them. The courses are usually wet and muddy. Shoes without an aggressive grip will slip and slide. Try climbing up a wet and muddy hillside in flat running shoes, you won't make much progress uphill.

In one of my first races, I got away with regular sneakers for a 5k Mud run. They unfortunately did not make it back home after the race though. A good trail running shoe will be adequate. You most likely will not need the lightest sneaker or most aggressive lugs/tread for a 5k race. Just a shoe that won't slip and slide in muddy terrain.

Most terrain in the races can be broken down to a few categories:

- Dry
- Packed/flat
- Loose/Gravel
- Hills
- Muddy

- Rocky
- Wet
- Field/grassy/trail

You will need to know the combination of the terrain to have the right shoe for the job. Consider the weather before and during the race. Did it rain or will it rain while you will be on the course? If so, you will need a shoe with drainage. And dry shoes to change into after the race.

Anticipate more mud than sand? Will you be going uphill? Then you will need a more aggressive lug to keep traction as well as a good lace system to keep the shoe on your foot. In the American Northeast there are some courses that have clay mixed into the mud. This type of terrain can suck the shoe right off your foot. Some racers find themselves finishing the race with one shoe.

Is the race on a mountain? Are there lots of technical switchbacks? Most likely there will be so you might want a shoe with good shank and ankle support. Especially if you tend to roll your ankle while running on rolling trails.

Footwear suggestions based on race type:

Here I will further break down the type of shoes and features needed for the race you will be doing. It is my hope to make you more aware of what is needed based on race type. Feel free to jump around to the race type you will be running.

- **Stadium/Urban Race**

Terrain: Dry, Packed/Flat, Concrete

Running sneakers are fine for these. Any functional fitness gym sneaker will work well.

- **5k-10k Trail OCRs**

Terrain: Muddy, Rocky, loose, field/trail

For these races you will need good drainage and laces, A shank guard will be good to have to protect your feet from rocks. I developed plantar fasciitis running on a very rocky and technical trail in a shoe that did not have any shank guard.

If you have poor ankles, then a shoe with heel and ankle support will be good to protect you from potentially rolling an ankle.

The weight of a shoe can start to be a factor in these races. If you plan on moving fast even a few extra grams will start to be noticeable when the shoes fill with mud and water. Be sure to try on a few different types of shoes. Most trail shoes will list their weight.

Shoe Features to Look For

Here I will be breaking down each feature of the shoes and why they are important to an Obstacle Course Racer.

- **Quick Draining/Drying**

OCRs go through dry, muddy and wet terrains. Running in wet shoes and socks that do not drain is downright miserable and will slow you down physically and mentally. A good pair of shoes will drain well and each step you take should push water out the sides to help dry the inside. This feature is a must have.

- **Lacing System**

I rarely find that I need a particular lacing system. If long laces feel like they get in the way or your laces often come undone there are some aftermarket systems to replace or add onto your shoes. Make sure that the shoelaces themselves are grippy and do not come undone easily. Replace the laces if needed. In long races your feet will swell. Make sure you can adjust the tightness or position of the laces if needed.

Type of Lugs/Bottoms

Different terrain will require varying heights and aggressiveness of your lugs on the bottom of the shoes. Below I will describe the uses of each type of ug and the terrain they are good for.

- **Flat or low height lugs**

  Packed Trail, fire roads, fields, low elevation, small or rolling hills. These low lugs are great for beginner racers. They feel like road runners and can be used on hard packed roads for short distances.

- **Moderate height lugs**

  Mixed trail: loose dirt, mud or slippery terrain, Going In and out of water, Switchbacks, some elevation, light rocky terrain. These are great for racers with some muddy elevation. You will feel very connected to the ground running up slick inclines.

- **Aggressive, big lugs**

  Mostly wet terrain, lots of mud, very slippery, lots of grip needed for traction, low rocky terrain, Multiple aggressive inclines and declines. Great for fast hikers. Some companies make an ultra-light/aggressive lug shoe for fell runners that need maximum traction uphill in rainy conditions. These are best for experienced racers.

- **Shank/Rock Guard**

  A shank or rock guard helps protect the bottom of the feet from sharp rocks or impact trauma. It is in the shoe under the arch/midfoot. Highly recommended for any rocky or mountainous terrain but not needed for flat or field type terrain. A rock guard is particularly good at helping stave off plantar fasciitis. If you already experience plantar fasciitis, I highly recommend having a shank/rock guard.

- **Ankle/Heel Support**

   Some shoes have ankle support, and some do not. Generally, the lighter and faster the shoe, the less support and stability the shoe will have. If you have weak ankles or tend to roll your ankle easily on the trail you will want a more laterally stable shoe. This may include a stiff back and higher mid top opening and more lacing.

- **Construction Material**

   The material for an OCR shoe is very important. For wet and/or muddy conditions you will want the shoe to drain water as efficiently as possible. For hot climates you will want the shoe to be breathable. For rocky terrain you will want the outside to be durable and be able to withstand abrasions and rocks. For cold climates the shoe should be able to help keep your feet warm and dry. If it is cold and wet, then look for a line of trail shoes that utilize Gore-Tex™ type of material. An upper that is waterproof or resistant to keep you dry. Remember that the more waterproof the shoe is the less breathable and flexible it will be.

Clothing

- **Shirts**

   The type of shirt or layers of shirts will be dependent on the weather and climate of the race. Some racers forgo shirts and instead run shirtless or in just a racing sports bra top.

- **Material type**

   You will want to wear a moisture wicking type of fabric. Companies like Under Armour and Nike make a great base layer tech shirt for racing. The material needs to be quick drying and not get heavy when wet. Cotton is not advised for any OCR race, avoid at all costs. The cotton shirts will get wet and heavy with mud and weigh you down as well as get caught on obstacles.

- **Sleeves**

Long sleeve, short sleeves, sleeveless, or tank? The length of the sleeve will depend on the weather and your comfort factor. I advise a long sleeve technical shirt for cool weather especially if there is water. The longer sleeves can also help reduce cuts from brush and obstacles. I sometimes wear a short sleeve race shirt over the long sleeve technical shirt.

Pants/Shorts

- **Shorts vs Pants**

This choice is entirely up to you, the racer. What are you most comfortable in? Do you get hot running? What will the weather and temperature be? Are you okay getting scrapes and scratches on your legs?

The important thing is to make sure that whichever you choose will not hold onto water. Make sure the shorts or pants are made for running sports. Avoid basketball shorts or any type of shorts or pants with long loose material. If you want pockets, make sure that they zip close. Open pockets tend to get caught on obstacles and hold mud.

- **Shorts**

What type of shorts are best to wear for a race? There are high cut, mid-thigh and knee length shorts. Running shorts and compression shorts. One thing to think about is the tighter the shorts are to the body the less chance they will have to get caught on obstacles.

It is important to try a few different types during training to find what you like best. You may not like the tightness of compression or "booty" shorts and prefer looser running shorts. You may need pockets to put things inside, some running shorts do not have pockets or if they do may not be big enough for your gear.

The material should be light and quick drying. Make sure they have a draw string to tie tight if they are loose. Also, test out how they feel wet while running. Make sure they do not chafe in unexpected areas.

- **Pants**

  While running pants and tights are great for training runs, they do not work for a race. It is best to wear compression pants, running tights, or crops.

- **Compression pants**

  The idea behind compression pants is that they help move blood flow throughout the legs. Because of their tightness on the body not everyone will like them. I personally have found that compression pants led to a greater chance of cramping in my legs. While others have found the opposite to be true. Compression pants are made as an under garment and generally do not include pockets. Different brands will have a slightly different fit so experimentation may be needed.

  I would like to suggest that you wear shorts over compression pants or at least wear racing underwear under the pants. In a few races I had the pleasure of being behind a racer who had their pants caught on barbed wire across their rear end. They were not wearing underwear and had to finish the race with their backside exposed to the world.

- **Running tights/crops**

  These can be weather or preference dependent. There are many female racers that prefer running tights to shorts. They are usually built with pockets and come in different thickness weights. So, you can get heavier ones for colder weather or lighter ones for warm weather.

- **Socks**

  Your everyday socks will not cut it for a muddy OCR. Socks are generally made in cotton, synthetic and wool material. Cotton is to be avoided. Synthetic or wool blends will be the best option for races. Some brands make OCR specific synthetic compression socks for muddy races. For longer and colder races, a wool racing/running sock may be best as it will stay warm while wet. Hiking wool socks are too thick.

For most races you will want a quick drying sock that has moisture wicking. This will help avoid blisters. If there is rope climbing in the race, I suggest long locks that cover the shins. You do not want to get rope burn on your shins and then run through muddy, possibly infected water with an open wound.

Hydration Systems

Hydration systems are ways to carry water during a race. The type of system you will use will be determined by the racecourses distance, elevation, water stations and your level of water, caloric, and electrolyte needs. Hydration systems are usually a requirement for most races, even short ones, an exception being the urban stadium races where there may be water fountains.

Water Packs

Hydration backpacks are extremely helpful on races 10k and above. You can pack extra food and clothing if needed. Some high elevation races will have various changes in weather/temperature throughout the race and you may need a warm layer for the top of a mountain. For races longer than 3-4 hours you will need multiple fueling options to keep with you and a pack makes it easy to take everything you need with you.

Avoid one with tubing or material that could get caught on barbed wire, trees, or climbing obstacles. My racing partner and I watched in dismay once when his mouthpiece got stuck on barbed wire, ripped off and all his water sprayed out all over him mid-way in a race. Pull on the mouthpiece, if you can take it off you will need to secure it or get a different model

Check the tubing delivery system, make sure that mud/debris will not get the mouthpiece dirty or that it is easy to clean. Newer style packs are now coming with covers or guards to keep dirt out. Nothing like sucking on a dirty muddy mouthpiece mid race.

Check the zippers and make sure they will work with mud and dirt and stay closed during the race. For longer races you will want to make sure you can get the pack on and off to get food easily.

Try it on and make sure it fits your torso size. Adjust all the straps and jump up and down. Does it shift? Is the sternum strap too high? Is the waist strap at your waist? These are all things you must test out and dial in during training runs. You want to avoid the straps digging into your skin and opening a wound. Open wounds and mud will lead to infections. Try different shirts on as the pack may feel good with a t-shirt but not with a tank top.

Get used to carrying your pack. 16 fl oz of water = just over 1 lb of pack weight. Make sure you train multiple times with a full pack Even if you don't intend to drink all the water. This will help you adjust the pack to avoid back pain or discomfort when running.

Hydration Pack Sizes

Small:

- Water: 1 - 2 liters (32 or 70 fluid ounces): Small and compact. Shorter races
- Capacity: 5 liters (or less), Lightweight, low profile, Enough room for a few essentials or snacks
- 1+ hr. runs

Medium:

- Water: 2 liters or 2.5 liters (70 or 85 fluid ounces)
- Medium capacity. Use for races 5-10k depending on the water stations and conditions
- Capacity: Ranges 6 - 10 Liters, you will find most running packs in this range. Use for 10k+ races, Plenty of room for food and supplements
- 1.5 - 2.5 hr. runs

Large:

- Water: 3 liters or more (100 fluid ounces or more): Lots of capacity, and weight. Use for long slower paced races with little access to water stations and possible changes in weather.
- Capacity: 11+ liters, extra pockets, can carry clothes, food, and supplements
- 3+ hr. run/hikes

Running Vest

Running vests are relatively new in the OCR scene and a cross over from ultra-running where they have been used for years. Some vests are like hydration packs with a tube delivery system but are very low profile and limited in pack space.

Vests mainly use a bottle system instead of a bladder and tube. This keeps the weight on the front of the body and easy access to multiple types of hydrations. You can have one water and one with electrolytes or calories for fueling.

The running vests are great for long training runs. However, since the bottles are in the front you will need to test out if they get in the way of you completing obstacles such as the wall or rope climb.

Running Bottle

Recently there has been a big shift from hydration packs to bottles in the longer trail running community. This may partially be due to some races having security concerns such as marathons which no longer allow packs or vests. Bottles can be placed on the Hip, in a belt, in a quiver style pack or handheld for easy access.

Test out different options and find the one that fits your style. Some options can be cumbersome or challenging for longer distances. Due to the limited capacity of the single bottle, they are only good for races that provide multiple water stations.

Race Day Bag

Bringing a bag or backpack for race day can really make your experience better. Most races will charge for a bag check, but it is worth it to have stuff to change into right after the race and not have to get back to the car. Some parking for races is far enough away that you will take a shuttle from the parking to the race start.

What is a race bag?

This is a bag or backpack that you don't mind getting dirty or wet but will keep anything you put in it dry and clean.

What's in the bag?

Inside the bag you should have the following:

2 trash bags, one to put all your dirty clothes in and one to wrap around your bag if it is raining.

A full change of comfortable clothes for after the race: underwear, sweatpants or shorts, a sweatshirt or light racing jacket (in case of hypothermia), t-shirt, hat (if it's sunny), comfortable socks, a pair of sneakers or flip flops/sandals

A big towel to dry off and wrap around yourself to get changed in the changing tent.

Post-race snack or fuel and extra water. I like to keep a shaker bottle with a single serve packet of protein/carb mix for a post workout shake.

Bonus: A newer item on the market is something called a Dry Robe. This is essentially a large thick robe that is lined with fleece to keep you warm and can be used to change in.

There is nothing better than finishing a race, getting washed off and changed into comfortable clothing. You spent all that time preparing for the start line, make sure you are also ready for the finish line and the ride home.

Headphones and speakers

Music is great and can keep us moving and positive. It can be motivating and rhythmic. While they are great for training, I highly recommend against headphones or speakers on the course. Go enjoy the sounds of nature and your fellow racers and live in the moment.

However, some racers may have headphones and speakers on the course, mostly in the open waves. Rarely do I see them in any competitive heats unless it's a long type of race like an ultra-distance race.

Headphones and speakers can help you on course. Listening to music can keep you to stay on pace and pump you up. If it's the open heat and you feel you need the tunes, I say go for it. But one of the detriments is that you cannot hear when another runner is coming up behind you. Or if you are on a team, you cannot hear if anyone needs help. Open ear headphones are best for this so you can hear the music and the environment.

The other downside is that you will settle into a pace like the music you are listening to. This may be slower than the speed you can move at. So, make sure your playlist is also up to the task of the race.

5

TRAINING EXERCISES —
THE ESSENTIAL OCR MOVEMENTS

Photo: Tough Mudder Media Team, Athlete: R. Borgatti

Obstacle Course Races require a wide variety of movements, coordination and strength. A racer must be able to navigate rough terrain, mud and slick surfaces as well as be able to lift and carry heavy objects. They need to support and manipulate their body from various hanging obstacles. To do so requires a great strength to bodyweight ratio.

In this section we will be defining the essential movements that will help a racer be proficient on race day. These movements all have great carry over from the short races to longer mountain races. Be sure to incorporate them into your routine.

Warming Up

Performing a good and consistent warm up before each training session is vital and important. A good rule of thumb is that the shorter the workout, the longer the warmup. Each warmup should be slightly tailored towards a) the task or workout at hand and b) reducing, alleviating, or mitigating possible or existing injuries.

Warming up for sprints should look different than warming up for lifting. While there may be similarities in a warmup, only you know your body best and should give more attention to your specific areas that you know need to be paid attention too.

It is not uncommon to hear athletes do not feel warmed up until 1-1.5m into a race. If the race is only a 5K then you wasted half the race! Do your best to dial in a warmup that works for you and makes you feel ready at the start line.

Mobility/ROM Warm Up

Goal is to perform 10 reps, rotations or :30s hold each movement. The warmup focuses on the joints of the body and is a great way to start a gym focused workout.

- Ankle Circles
- Knee Circles

- Hip Circles
- Torso Rotation
- Windmills
- Good mornings
- Shoulder Circles
- Arm Circles
- Neck Circles
- Walking Quad Reach Stretch
- Deep Squats
- Cossack Squats

Ankle Circles:

Knee Circles:

Hip Circles:

Torso Rotations:

Windmills:

Good Mornings:

Shoulder Circles:

Arm Circles:

Neck Circles:

Quad Reach Stretch:

Deep Squats:

Cossack Squats:

OCR Specific Dynamic warm up:

These are movements that are designed to help warm up specific areas related to an OCR specific workout, obstacle work or even before a race. Do the movements slow and controlled. This warmup includes lateral movements that trail runners need to help strengthen the ankles and support structure.

- 200-400m easy Jog
- Jumping jacks x20
- Skiers x20
- Skaters x20
- Mtn climbers (L/R=1) x20
- Air Squats x20
- Jumping or walking lunges (L/R=1) x20
- Butt Kicks 20m (Fwd./backward)
- High Knees 20m (Fwd./backward)
- 5 Burpees
- 200-400m easy jog

Jumping Jacks:

Skiers:

Skaters:

Mountain Climbers:

Air Squats:

Walking Lunges:

Butt Kickers:

High Knees:

Burpee:

Footwork Drills

Include these footwork drills 2-4x per month. The goal is not the speed of the drills but coordination and consistency. Too many athletes place an emphasis on foot speed or how fast you can move from the beginning to the end.

What we really want to focus on for the OCR athlete is stability of the foot, ankle and knee. Agility drills help develop the ability to change direction and develop ground reaction speed. If you do not have an agility ladder you can make one on the ground with chalk or tape. Make a line of 10 squares each 1'x1' as a 10' ladder.

Agility ladder stepping

- in-in-out-out
- Start in front of ladder
- Step 1-2 feet inside
- Step 1-2 feet outside to each respective side
- Step 1-2 feet inside the next ladder hole, Cont...

- Lateral in-in-out-out
- Start on one side of the ladder (outside but parallel to ladder)
- Step forward 1-2 into the ladder
- Step back out 1-2 outside the ladder
- Step diagonally 1-2 to the next ladder hole, cont...

Zig Zag

- Start outside (left side of ladder), double step (right then left) in square
- Right foot goes outside square to the right side
- Step forward and left and Double step (Left then right) inside of next square
- Left foot goes outside square to the left side
- Repeat in a zig zag fashion

Crawling

Crawling movements are a mainstay in most Obstacle Races. From steep hill climbs and descents as well as over, under and through obstacles you may find yourself on all fours. In training they can be used as a mobility and flexibility tool as well as a conditioning exercise. I have found myself using each of these methods' multiple times during a race. From crawling under barbed wire to going down an extremely steep hill on my hands and feet.

The "A-B-C's" (Ape/Bear/Crab)

These movements are often compiled together because they can flow together. You can mix and match these three movements into a variety of combinations. Don't underestimate these movements or a combo of them. They can be great fun in a workout but are challenging over a long time.

Ape

The ape movement is a lateral quadruped crawl low to the ground. This is also sometimes called a Beast Hop.

- Start in a deep squat low to the ground
- Reach both hands to the side and on the ground
- Once hands are on the ground hop/skip your legs to the other side of your hands
- Repeat for 5 to 10 reps and then go back in the other direction to where you started

The Ape movement is great at building low crawl flexibility and movement in the hips and shoulders. Low crawls are a staple in the OCR world and the ape crawl will transfer to not only the ground but also vaulting low walls.

Bear

The Bear Crawl is a forward or backward contralateral quadruped movement. The athlete is facing the ground with their hands/feet under them. Beginners may have to keep the knees on the ground. We call that the Baby Crawl.

- Start with hands and knees on the ground
- Have a flat "tabled" back
- Lift knees 1-2 inches off the ground or until your shins are parallel to the ground
- Move the opposite hand and foot (contralateral) at the same distance and rate. Most people have an issue when they either reach too far with their hands or step too far with their feet. Small movements are best.
- Go 10 steps forward then 10 steps backward

The Bear crawl will help build stamina on the low crawls such as barbed wire and tube crawls but also directly helps the coordination and stamina for cargo net climbs as it is a very similar movement. A mistake most athletes make with this move is having the hips too high in the air. The hips and shoulders should be at similar heights. The back will be flat and parallel to the ground.

Crab

The crab crawl is a contralateral (opposite hand and leg moving at once) forward and backward crawl that helps develop shoulder flexibility, as well as Tricep and core strength. The athlete is facing the ceiling or sky and the hands/feet on the ground behind them.

- Start sitting on the ground with your hands behind you and feet on the ground.
- Lift your hips off the ground slightly
- Move your opposite hands and feet so you move forward. This does not need to be fast.
- For an added effect you can try to "pull" yourself forward with your heel as you move.
- Do 10 steps forward and backward

The Crab crawl is very beneficial for extreme downhill movement. Sometimes slopes are so steep that you will need to go down while sitting.

Army Crawl

The Army crawl is a contralateral low crawl using the arms and legs with the body fully on the ground. This is useful for low barbed wire crawls especially through muddy or slippery terrain. To be effective in using this crawl in a race you will need good hip/leg flexibility.

- Start laying down on the ground
- Prop your upper body up on your forearms, hips and legs stay on the ground. Head slightly up to look forward.
- Move right elbow/arm forward and bend left knee up towards hip level.
- Push with your feet and pull your body forward with your arms. Alternate arms/legs as you move forward.

The Army Crawl can be particularly tough on the elbows and knees. When training in a gym setting, cover these parts to avoid "rug burn" with excessive contact on rubber or turf flooring.

Lizard/Spiderman

The Lizard or sometimes called the Spiderman Crawl is a combination of a crawl and a push up. This move helps build low crawl mobility through the hips and arm strength to hold the body up.

- Start in a plank position
- Move the opposite arm and leg forward while staying as low to the ground as possible, like a lizard walk
- Here you can do a low push up, lower yourself to the ground and back up
- Next move the other opposite arm and leg forward and repeat

Rolling

Traverse Roll/Side Roll

Traverse or Side rolling is a very quick way to move forward under barbed wire for short distances. Side rolling is not recommended for long distances due to nausea and disorientation. As well, it becomes hard to notice potential objects such as rocks. If you have a hydration pack on it is recommended that you remove it and hold it in the front while rolling.

Some races explicitly state that they want you to take the pack with you for the obstacle and others do not require it. Do some training with your pack on so you know how to do it in a race.

- Start on your side, keep your arms tucked into your chest
- Roll sideways, watch out for rocks.
- Rest and switch sides periodically to reduce nausea

A good training drill for this roll comes from the gymnastics world. Start in the hollow body position and then roll to the side into a Superman position. The Hollow Body position is on your back with your arms/shoulders and legs off the ground. The Superman position is on your belly with arms/chest and legs off the ground.

Combat Roll

This is also called a shoulder roll. This is different from a tumbling gymnastics style roll. This roll goes across the back from shoulder to opposite hip to minimize the impact to the neck and spine.

This roll is useful for getting over soft obstacles like hay bales or helping you absorb the impact of an unexpected fall.

- Start on the floor on your knees. Use gymnastics mat at first
- Place one hand on the ground
- The other hand will now reach across your body between your hand and knee
- Lower yourself so the shoulder is on the ground
- Tuck your chin in
- Roll over the shoulder. You may need to push off with your feet to get over your shoulder. It's okay if you need to lift your knees off the ground.
- Stay tucked as you roll
- Stand up

Putting the Movements Together for Training

Training the crawls and rolls together can be a great way to create a fun warm up or a challenging indoor obstacle course. We can combine them together into a circuit for maximum effect

Roll, Crawl, Run sequence

Modify as needed for reps/distance. Add some variety by swapping different crawls or adding low crawl obstacles like string or rope to simulate barbed wire or boxes to hop over in between crawls.

- 2-4 side rolls

- 4 Army crawl (2/side)
- 4 Baby Crawl steps (2/side)
- 4 Bear Crawl steps (2/side)
- Get up into a run or sprint (10m)
- Repeat

Over, Under, and through

Setting up a small obstacle course can be creative and fun. My favorite is the one that incorporates climbing and crawling by using small obstacles to go over and under. These can be objects like boxes, benches, walls, fences or even horizontally placed PVC pipe or rope/string. Do your best to use your imagination to create various crawls and climbs in a combo.

- Vault over a low obstacle (ex: plyometrics Box)
- Crawl under obstacle using one of the crawls
- Set up some PVC pipe or rope horizontally above the ground at 12-24"
- Go through an obstacle like a large tube or window
- Land and go into a short sprint

Pulling

Pulling exercises are extremely fundamental to Obstacle Course racing. Most obstacles will require great pulling strength and conditioning. Many races incorporate the use of hanging obstacles to tax the racers grip, shoulders, biceps, Lats, and upper back. All of these areas are trained through various horizontal and vertical pulling movements. This tends to be the area most racers need improvement with.

Vertical Pulling:

Ring/TRX Rows

This is a great basic building block for building good pulling strength and keeping the core engaged while pulling. Start here if you are new to pulling movements or cannot do a bodyweight pull up.

Using a set of gymnastics rings, a suspension system or even a pair or ropes hold onto the ends.

- Bring the rings or handles to your chest
- Walk backwards until the bands are tight
- Keeping the rings and your body where they are, walk your feet forward until you feel a downward pull
- With your feet on the ground, lower your body backwards down to an angle.
- The angle to the ground will determine the difficulty or load of this movement. The more horizontal your body and forward your feet are the harder it is.
- Pull yourself up to the rings or handles

Single Arm Row w/ rings

This row variation starts in a contracted position holding onto a ring or handle and angling your body back like a full ring row above.

- Using a single gymnastics ring, a suspension system handle or even a climbing rope.
- Bring the ring or handle to your chest
- Walk backwards until the band is tight
- Keeping the ring and your body where they are, walk your feet forward until you feel a slight downward pull
- With your feet on the ground, lower your body down.
- Keep the body and shoulders rigid and squared. Do not let your other side drop farther than the supporting shoulder. The hips should also stay tight and not dip towards the ground at the extension of the row.

- The angle to the ground will determine the difficulty or load of this movement. The more horizontal your body and forward your feet are the harder it is.
- Pull yourself up to the ring or handle
- Add in an optional reach with the other arm. This simulates reaching for a monkey bar or other support ring.

Scapular Pulls

This is a great shoulder and upper back strengthening exercise. This movement helps create the correct type of hanging strength that we need for obstacles like monkey bars. This can be down leaning back on rings and hanging from a pull up bar.

- Hang from a pull up bar with hands just slightly wider than the shoulders
- Let the shoulders go loose and come towards the ears
- Keep the arms straight
- Tighten up the shoulders and pull the body towards the pull up bar, the shoulders should pull away from the ears and the shoulder blades/scapula will pull down
- Lower back down and repeat

Narrow Grip Pull Up

This is a pull up with the hands at or inside the width of the shoulders. The palms will be facing away from the body. This pull up tends to be more arm/bicep focused than upper back.

- Place hands on pull up bar, hands are inside the shoulders
- Engage core/ab muscles
- Pull body towards bar until chin is over the bar

Wide Grip Pull Up

This is a pull up with arms wider than shoulders. This requires more Latissimus Dorsi (Lat) engagement to complete the pull up.

- Place hands on pull up bar wider than shoulders
- Engage core/ab muscles
- Pull body towards pull up bar until chin is over bar

Horizontal Pulling:

These pulls are fantastic strength endurance builders. In a race there may be tire or sled pulls in the mud. Be sure to engage your core and use your legs. If you use too much low back for the pulling it could lead to low back soreness.

Sled Pulls

Forward/Backward

To do this properly you will need to use a harness or rope attached to a weight sled. If you are new to sled pulling, start off using a light weight. You will feel this the next day in your hamstrings and glutes if done properly. It is a great way to strengthen the legs and core without loading up the low back.

- Face forward (away from the sled) or backward (towards the sled)
- You can either walk or run/jog facing forward or backward. This will also depend on the weight on the sled and what intent you have for the workout. I suggest starting with walking.
- If walking backwards keep the arms straight.

Horizontal

Horizontal sled pulls are great to build up the lateral strength of the hips and legs. Very useful for uphill running on bad terrain where you may be moving side to side up a steep hill or using the "French" technique of mountain climbing.

- Attach a sled harness/belt to your hips and a sled, you will need a rope or similar attachment that is 6+ feet.
- Face perpendicular to the sled
- Lean away from the sled and start walking, crossing your feet over each other.
- Switch sides

Arm pull/walk

This is an explosive upper body pulling movement. Make sure that the sled can move well such as on turf. This is NOT a maximal movement. Use light to moderate weight. Use a strap that has handles such as a TRX or suspension trainer or loops. You can do a narrow or a wide pull.

- Walk backwards away from sled with handles, until the slack is taken out of the strap.
- Straighten arms, pull sled towards you
- Walk back until line is straight again then Pull

Row Movements

Bent Over Row

This movement can be done with a barbell, dumbbells or kettlebells. For Obstacle Race training we suggest using a dumbbell or kettlebell as you can work on each side separately. Most obstacles require a single arm to be able to support your whole-body weight.

- Bend over at the waist with a slight bend in the knees.

- Your back should be as close to parallel with the ground as possible and should be straight and tight. Be sure not to round the lower back.
- If doing a one-handed row, place the other hand on a box or bench for support and balance.
- Pull your hand(s) to your chest, elbow towards the ceiling. The hand should come to the bottom of your rib cage with the forearm being perpendicular to the ground. Do not bend the wrist at the top.
- At the top of the pull to make sure you are squeezing the muscles between the shoulder and the spine.
- Lower the weight back down to full arm extension.
- Beware not to overextend the arm at the shoulder joint. Keep the shoulder packed tight at the bottom.

Single DB Bent Over Row:

Double DB Bent Over Row:

Barbell Bent Over Row:

Single Arm DB Row w/ rotation

This row variation is like the Single DB bent over row above. It adds the extra rotation movement at the end. This helps build rotational torso strength into the pull. Like the way we would pull on the Herc Hoist at a Spartan Race.

- With one DB/KB, Pull the weight to the chest.
- The weight should touch the bottom of the rib cage. When this happens, rotate the torso to look at the wall to your side or ceiling.
- Rotate back towards the floor and lower the weight.
- Caution: go slow and use a light weight, a fast rotation could lead to injury.

Banded Pulls

Face Pulls

There are a few variations to this pull. This pull utilizes a rubber workout band to help develop the smaller muscles of the upper back. Use a light to moderate resistance band (½ - ¼ inch thick)

- Place a workout band around a pole, hold onto each end with the middle behind a post or pole.
- Step back until there is tension in the band
- Keep the body straight, pull the elbows back at the same height of the shoulders.
- Your hands should pull back towards your face.
- You can vary the height of the band as well as the distance between your hands.
- The band should be light enough to work on multiple high rep sets (ex. 3x20 pulls)

Horizontal Pull Apart

Vertical Pull Apart

Pull/Push Downs

- This requires you to attach a resistance band to a pull up bar or a secure structure above you.
- This move works the triceps and shoulders. This move is great for a finisher at the end of a workout or training.
- Once attached above grab the band with both hands.
- Secure the elbow to the side of the body, try not to move the elbows forward or backward.
- Push down on the band, straightening the arm down. Bring the hands back up to 90 degrees. Keep the band under control, do not relax the arm and allow the band to "snap" back up.
- The band should be light enough in resistance to allow you to do multiple high rep sets. Work up to 100 reps (ex. 4x25 or 2x50 sets)

Rope Pulls

Herc Hoist

This is a race obstacle as well as a strength exercise. The Hercules or Herc Hoist is a vertical weighted pull. The rope is approximately ⅝ thickness and is run through a pulley that is suspended 15' to 20' off the ground.

- You can attach the pulley closer to the ground if needed in training. One end of the rope is attached to a weight. This weight could be a sandbag, a kettlebell, chains, bucket or rocks etc., but in a race, it is a heavy sandbag approximately 70 to 100#s. Make sure you measure the weight you are using.

- Beginners should start at a light weight; I suggest that 20-30 lbs. is a good place to start. Work up to being able to lift between 60 - 100 lbs. 15-20ft in the air.
- This pull is best done seated on the ground with something to brace yourself against. You can use your first pull to sit on the ground. Once you are sitting on the ground you pull the rope hand over hand until the weight reaches the pulley.
- Lower the weight hand over hand. Do not let the rope slide through your hands or completely let go of the rope and drop the weight.

Rope Climbs

Sit to Stand

The sit to stand rope climb is a great way for beginners to develop the grip strength and pulling strength needed for a rope climb. This can also be a great conditioning drill for more intermediate/advanced racers to safely pull vertically on a rope under fatigue without the fear of falling.

- Start by standing in front of the climbing rope. The rope should be just a few inches to ½ ft away from your body.

- Sit down on the ground and grab the rope. There should be an angle to the rope. This is approximately a 20 to 30-degree angle.
- Note: if your feet travel past the anchor point you will have a hard time pulling yourself up to standing properly and will have to arch your back excessively. This may cause you to lose balance as well. When you grab the rope, your feet should be an arm's length from the rope.
- Beginners start by sitting up straight with legs bent. Intermediate and advanced athletes can lay down flat on the ground. Intermediate athletes can bend the knees. Advanced athletes will keep the legs straight.
- Engage your core (tighten up your abs and midsection) before you start pulling.
- Start pulling on the rope until you are standing. You should not bend your spine to get up. If you must bend, your feet may be too close to the rope.
- To return to the ground, have a good grip on the rope and lean back. Keep your core tight. Lower yourself down hand over hand. Beginners can bend at the knees and waist and sit down. Intermediates can bend at the knees and advanced will keep the body straight.

Anchoring

There are two main anchoring techniques racers can use to climb a rope. The Spanish Wrap and the J-Hook. Both will work to get up the rope. However, the J-Hook is a much faster version for getting up the rope.

I find the S-wrap to be more cumbersome to re-anchor and requires more practice to be efficient at it for racing. However, the S-wrap can provide a more secure feeling for some racers. You will need to practice both to see which one works best for you. To learn the anchoring methods both will follow the same method to learn:

- Start by sitting just behind the hanging rope. You can use a box or a bench, but it should be a bit higher off the ground than a normal chair to give your legs some room.
- Use one of the anchoring methods as described below while sitting. Practice wrapping and unwrapping the rope to get used to the movement.
- Once you feel you have a good solid anchor work on standing up on the rope while anchored. Repeat until your feet do not slip, and you can stand up entirely.
- Test the wrap out. I like to test the anchoring out by taking a hand off the rope and waving. Try both hands, one hand at a time.

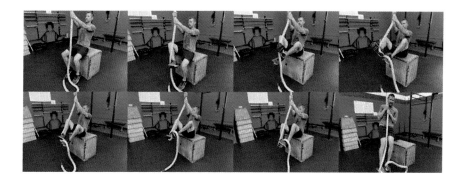

The S-Wrap (Spanish Wrap)

This anchoring technique is usually the safest and easiest for a beginner to learn and understand. Most athletes have initial success with this method but as they fatigue it can get increasingly more difficult to maintain due to having to completely release the rope and re-wrap the anchor every time you ascend the rope. This method is not meant for speed, and it is easy to lose the rope or have it get bunched up when you are re-wrapping the anchor.

- The rope will start in your centerline. Grab the rope with both hands. Your dominant hand will be on top to start.
- Use your dominant leg for the wrap.
- Your leg starts on the outside of the rope, wrap your foot in front of the rope and then behind the rope.
- The rope should now drape over the arch of your foot still in your centerline.

The J-Hook

This is the anchoring technique for many racers for good reason. It's fast to set up, fast to ascend, and fast to descend. It is also very easy to secure if you are able to jump up the rope. The only downside to this technique is that it is not as secure as the s-wrap, but for racing this is not an issue since we are not climbing very high.

- Start with the rope in your centerline in front of you. Hold onto the rope, dominant hand on top.
- Take your dominant leg and pick your knee up to your waist. Your knee will be on the outside of the rope and your foot on the other side of the rope. This should put the rope in the crease of your ankle and foot.

- Rotate your leg outward (external rotation) so your shin is as perpendicular to your body as possible. If you do not rotate your leg your knee will get in the way of the rope, the rope will not align properly with your ankle, and the rope will not slide properly when you go to re-anchor the rope.
- It may get bunched up on the top of your foot the first time you try to do a second pull. You will essentially be picking up the rope and not repositioning the anchor higher up the rope. Practice sliding your ankle up and down the rope to make sure you have the action correct.
- Once you have the dominant leg action down, we can work on the anchoring.

Rope Climb (w/ anchoring)

The rope climb can be a challenging obstacle on the course. The rope will be wet and muddy and make holding onto it difficult. But in training we can break it down and learn to climb efficiently in a safe and clean manner. I suggest wearing long pants and/or long socks for training the rope climb or some sort of shin protection.

To rope climb efficiently we will need to learn and practice the anchor, the stand, curl up and the re-anchor. Try it with dry shoes and wet shoes.

Pushing

Pushing movements are not as commonly found in an obstacle race yet. We are starting to see more sleds, wall balls and tire flips in some races. Incorporating pushing exercises is important to help develop a strong upper body and offset all the pulling that is done in a race. These movements keep the shoulder girdle strong as well as helping build a stable core.

Push ups

Pushups are a staple of every exercise routine. They are simple and can be done almost anywhere. They can be modified in a variety of ways from wall pushups to knee pushups to incline pushups. There is always a way to make them easier or harder. Below I will list a few variations to add into your routine.

- Close (Tricep)
- Hands are placed inside the shoulders in front of the chest
- Elbows stay in close to the body

Neutral

Hands are placed in front of the shoulders or a hand width outside the shoulders

Wide

Hands are placed 1-2 hand widths outside the shoulders to the side.

Offset

One hand is placed above the chest line and the other at the chest line. This is a staggered set up and should alternate which hand is above and below the chest line.

Staggered Knee to elbow

This is related to the Lizard or spiderman crawl. Stagger the hands like the offset push up. On the lower hand side bring your knee to rest on the elbow. You may need to lean a bit and move your other hands/feet to get a good balance position. Lower yourself to the ground, then alternate sides.

Lateral Walking/Traveling Push up

Do a push up, while in a plank walk your hands to one side. You may need to cross your hands. Keep your feet where they are. Once you are back in a plank position do a pushup. Walk your hands back and repeat.

I like to add in a raised surface to walk my hands over like a bumper plate or yoga block.

Burpees

Burpee

The Burpee is a dynamic compound exercise where you drop down to the ground and then get up and jump. They are a staple of Spartan Race who incorporate 15-30 reps as a penalty for failing some obstacles.

How to do a Burpee

- The goal is to get to the ground and then back up quickly.
- Here is 1 rep:
- Start standing
- Squat down and put hands on the ground
- Jump or walk feet back to a plank
- Lower quickly to the ground
- Do a push up and jump feet forward towards hands
- Stand up and jump with arms over head

This movement is loved and loathed in every workout program it is a part of. It is hard when done fast or slow, in small sets or large. The burpee is a full body movement and can be used to develop explosive power or cardiovascular conditioning. Part of the reason most find the movement so difficult is that it constricts your ability to breathe during movement and can affect your blood pressure going down and up so fast.

Burpee tips:
- I like to have my feet wider than my hips. This helps me get to the ground without having to really squat or having my knees in the way.
- Breathe in and hold while you go down and breathe out on the way up.
- Keep your core tight/braced. Keeping your breath in will help with this. This will reduce bending/flexing your low back and

reduce low back pain/discomfort. This will also help you get off the ground and not "snake" or "yoga" push up your body off the ground.

Up/Down

The Up/Down is a good entry point into burpees. It does not require a push up or a jump.

- Squat down, go into a plank (Squat Thrust), hop back in and stand. If needed you can step back/in instead of jumping.

Break Down Burpee

Doing each part of the burpee with a 1-2 sec pause and focusing on each part as its own movement. This is great for warmups before a workout with burpees.

- Squat
- Plank
- Push up
- Squat
- Jump

Burpee Broad Jump

Like a burpee but instead of a vertical jump you perform a forward broad jump. This helps develop power.

Burpee Box Jump

In front of a plyo box do a burpee, jump up onto the box then step down. A more demanding version of the burpee. It is okay to take a step forward before the jump. You do not need to jump from where you stand up.

Lateral Burpee

Instead of a vertical jump you perform a horizontal jump. This is usually over an object like a line on the ground, hurdle or barbell.

Burpee Pull up

Under a pull up bar do a burpee, when you jump grab the pull up bar and do a pull up.

If you are new to these, start with a pull up bar below your reach. If you raise your arms above your head the bar should be between your elbow and wrist. Test it out with a jumping pull up. If you cannot get your chin over the bar (aim for the bar to touch the top of your chest) then you need a lower bar. More advanced athletes will have the bar approximately 6" above their reach.

Medicine Ball

The medicine ball is a versatile tool that can help develop upper body explosiveness, shoulder strength and core strength. This movement is best incorporated into training sessions as a conditioning tool. Some stadium style races are incorporating more medicine balls as part of their stations.

Chest pass (Horizontal Toss)

- Standing in front of a concrete wall. Start at a bit farther than your arm length until you get an idea of how hard you can throw the ball. The harder you can "pass" the ball the further away you can get.
- Feet can be two positions. Parallel (or neutral stance) or staggered (throwing stance). If you are in a staggered stance, be sure

to switch which foot is forward. There are some variations where you can be in a lunge or kneeling position instead of standing.

- Hold a med ball at your chest and push/pass the ball forward at the wall. If you are close you may be able to catch the ball off the wall.

Rotational

The rotational throw develops core rotational strength as well as hand-eye coordination.

- Start facing perpendicular to the wall (sideways)
- The ball can be thrown a few ways:

Chest pass

- Same as above, can add a few steps before the trough to develop power.

Overhead

- Holding the ball behind your head, when you turn and face the wall step forward with your lead leg and throw the ball.

Swing pass

- Holding the med ball down, arms are straight, and the ball is "hanging" in your hands. As you rotate the arms will swing like a golf swing. Release the ball when the hips are facing the wall.
- Turn, face the wall and throw the ball

Wall Ball (Vertical Toss)

This pass variation requires the whole body as well as proper breathing.

- You will need a target above on a wall or post you can toss the ball at. Most workout routines use a 9' or 10' target.
- Different weights of medicine balls will require a different distance away from the wall. In general, start about an arm's length away from the wall and adjust if needed. It is best to start with a lighter ball (8-10#) and work up to a heavier ball (14-20#)
- Start holding the ball against your chest, hands on the side of the med ball. Have your feet in a hip width or slightly wider hip width stance. This is a squat stance.
- While holding the med ball, squat down while keeping the ball and chest level. Keep looking forward to the wall. If you see the floor your chest drops too much.
- Stand up powerfully. As you stand up quickly, extend your arms and throw the ball at the target. This should look like a small jump even though your feet may stay on the ground. Leave your hands in the air to catch the ball
- When the ball comes down to your hands, absorb the impact by retracting your arms and the ball back to your chest and using that momentum to send you back into your next squat.

6

OBSTACLE STRENGTH WORK

Photo: R. Borgatti, Athlete: N.DeMarco

Strength work for the Obstacle Course athlete or those training to run their first race is a must. I have often found that certain areas of strength can be the difference between just surviving a race and having a great race.

The most underutilized areas of strength for beginner athletes are upper back pulling strength, uphill climbing strength (Quads, calves and glutes) and grip strength. Prioritizing these areas during training for a race.

In this chapter you will be introduced to the best movements to incorporate into your training routine. It is highly recommended to work with a fitness professional, coach or trainer to learn the basics of these movements when possible.

Squats

Squats are utilized in almost every strength program there is and for good reason. Strong legs make strong athletes. From bodyweight only to weighted squats there is a version for just about everyone.

Air Squat

(Bodyweight, no external load)

This squat is just sitting down and standing up. It is an essential move for everyday life. When done correctly it can help improve sports performance and improve your quality of life into old age.

- To start, first set the feet slightly wider than the hips. The stance should feel comfortable. Your spine will be straight and standing tall.
- The squat movement starts in the hips. Most people start by bending the knees first but this is incorrect for proper movement especially if you ever want to add an external load to the movement.
- While keeping your spine straight and core tight push your hips back behind you. This should start to transfer your weight towards your heels.

- We will start to sit down and bend the knees. Make sure that the knees are pointing in the same direction as your toes. The knees should not cave in towards each other.
- Lower your hips down so that they are parallel with your knees or just below. Be mindful to keep your chest up and lower back straight. Reach your arms out in front to help keep your balance.
- When you start to stand up, push through your heels and not your toes/ball of the foot. Engage your glutes on the way up. Stand tall to finish

Goblet Squat

(Credit: Coach Dan John)

The Goblet squat is one of the best and safest variations of squats. It has great carryover to OCR due to helping increase ROM in the hips and upper body tension to hold the kettlebell. This squat variation is credited to strength coach Dan John.

- Start by holding the kettlebell at chest level by the horns. The horns are the vertical part of the handle.
- Keep the elbows close to the body.
- Sit down into a squat, keeping your chest up and core tight. Do your best to not round your back. Keep the legs engaged and do not let the pelvis get tucked under.
- Stand back up by pressing your feet into the ground and keeping your core tight.

Split Squats

The split squat is a unilateral lower body exercise. You are putting most of the load or work on one leg. This is important because most of the work in an OCR involves only one leg at a time such as running and climbing.

This movement can be done with just bodyweight (no external load) or can be loaded up with many variations such as dumbbells, kettlebells, sandbags and barbells. The load can also be distributed in different ways. Weight hanging down by the side, up at the chest in a zercher or goblet squats, In a front rack or back squat position. Even holding something overhead can add to more core stabilization.

The split squat is different from a lunge in that once the feet are placed in position they do not move until the reps are finished. As opposed to a lunge where you would bring the feet back underneath the hips every rep.

- Place one foot forward and one foot back like a lunge. Do not stack the feet in a line, this will cause you to have a poor base for balance and may fall over. Have the feet slightly apart from the center.
- Lower rear knee to the ground, keep your chest up and shoulders over the hips. The rear knee does not have to touch the ground, but the front knee should get as close to 90 degrees as is comfortable.
- Press the legs into the ground and raise up as high as is comfortable. Do not move the feet

- unless you need to adjust in order to finish all the reps. Repeat lowering to the ground.

Bulgarian (Raised leg)

This is a more challenging variation of the split squat. The rear leg will be elevated off the ground. This could be up on a bench or box. They even make special elevated rollers for this movement.

The Bulgarian or raised version puts more load on the front leg and adds in a degree of balance. Make sure that the front foot is set in place first then reach back with the rear foot to place it on the bench or box.

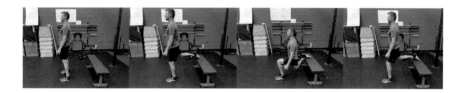

Front Squats

Front squats are any squat that has an external load in the frontal plane. This can be across the shoulders or held in the hands in front of the body. There are many variations of the front squat.

The front squat is great for OCR because of the cross over to all the frontal carries that are in races such as the sandbag or bucket carry.

Barbell Front Squat
- Start with a Barbell in a squat rack just below shoulder height
- Place hands just outside shoulder width on the barbell
- Step forward and under the barbell. Allow your hands to rotate, keep your grip light or open your hands. Push your elbows forward so they are now pointing away from your body and the barbell is resting on top of your shoulders.
- If you have difficulty raising your elbows in front of the barbell, try to release your last two fingers off the barbell

- Once the barbell is on the shoulders, stand up and lift the barbell out of the rack and take 2 steps back.
- The feet will be under the shoulders or just wider than your hips. This stance may be different for you as its dependent on your anatomy
- Keep the core braced, elbows up/pointing forward and gaze forward
- Squat down by first pushing the hips back slightly, knees may push out laterally a bit.
- Keep the spine upright and do not let the upper back round forward.
- Stand back up, keep the elbows as high as you can as you return to standing

Dumbbell Front Squat
- The DB Front squat is like the barbell front squat above.
- The dumbbells are held perpendicular to the body, one head of the dumbbell rests on the shoulders while the hands hold the rest of the dumbbell.
- Keep the elbows out in front, do not let them drift out to the side.

KB Front Rack

The Kettlebell Front Rack squat is perhaps one of the hardest variations of the front squat and has a high degree of crossover for the OCR athlete. Therefore, it is an excellent version for any OCR athlete to incorporate into their routine.

Warning: Make sure you do not have a watch, wearable fitness device or jewelry on your wrist.

There is a single KB and double KB version

- Clean the KB to the shoulder.
- If you do not know the proper way to clean the KB, please seek out a certified KB coach to show you.
- Your thumb will be against your chest close to your sternum
- The KB "bell" will rest in the space between your forearm and bicep
- The elbow should be slightly raised and off your torso.
- Once the Bell(s) are in the front rack position breathe in and tighten your core
- Squat down
- Keep your torso upright as you descend/ascend,
- Keep your shoulders pulled back slightly and tight as the KBs will tend to make you slouch forward and cave the shoulders in toward the chest.

Zercher Squat

The Zercher squat is a favorite for OCR training. I like to use a sandbag, but a barbell is the most common implement.

- Start by placing the barbell or sandbag in the crook of the elbow. Your forearms will be perpendicular to the ground. Squat down and back up. There may be some slight rounding of the upper back on this lift. You will need a very tight core and keep the shoulders rising at the same rate as your hips, so you do not bend forward.
- Some warning, this lift can cause discomfort on the elbow and is advised to have a long sleeve shirt on or padding on the barbell.

Back Squats

The back squat is a squat with an external load on the upper back/ Shoulders.

There are 2 variations of the barbell back squat: high bar and low bar. For our purposes we will only be going over the high bar back squat.

Barbell Back Squat

The barbell back squat is considered the king of the strength lifts. A dedicated squat program will get you strong and help build mental toughness. For the OCR athlete though this comes with some tradeoffs. Namely, sore legs, back and knees. I advise most athletes to only include serious back squatting (above 70% effort/weight of a 1 rep max) in the off season as part of a strength building phase.

The strength building phase would be 6-8 weeks max. Heavy back squat sessions will make your legs sore and tired and need adequate recovery. When training for long hill races I like to do a style of run "brick" training of squatting and running to get used to "heavy" feeling legs.

- The Back squat starts in a squat rack with the barbell just below shoulder height. Step under the bar and place it across your upper back. Tighten your shoulders back and together to create a shelf of muscle for the bar to rest on. The bar should not be pressing into/against bone. Stand up and step back out of the rack with the barbell across your upper back/traps.
- Set feet slightly wider than hip width, about shoulder width. Weight should be centered on the midfoot and heels, not the toes.
- Start to squat by breathing in, tightening your core and pushing your hips back and lowering them down. Keep your chest up, a slight lean forward or downward gaze is okay. Do not let the spine flex as you squat. Full range of motion is the hips being slightly below parallel at the bottom.
- When ascending, press the heels into the ground, keep the chest up and squeeze the glutes towards the top. Breath out about ¾ of the way up. Watch out for the knees collapsing or pulling inwards.

Sandbag Squat

This is the same as above but with a sandbag across the back or on one shoulder. This is a bit more applicable to the OCR athlete as you will be carrying one to two sandbags up and down hills in races. Use this variation in season. Practice across the upper back and on one shoulder, switching between left and right sides.

Box Squat

This is the version that I like the best and can help build some serious explosiveness out of the bottom of the squat.

- Set up a very sturdy wooden or metal box (a plyometric box) behind you where you are going to squat. The box height should be such that the crease of your hip is at the same height as your knee. To make it harder to sit a bit lower or easier a bit higher. Most people will be around a 12" box.

- Start the Back squat as you normally would, this can be body weight only or with an external load.
- Step back into the box and set your feet. Your heels should be close or touching the box. Sit back onto the box.
- When you sit onto the box keep your core tight and spine straight. Do not relax on the box or slouch your shoulders. Keep your legs engaged and do not come down hard onto the box. Pause briefly on the box and then push your heels down hard and squeeze your glutes as you stand up quickly. Do your best to stand up as vertically as you can. Do not fold or lean forward (especially if you have weight on your shoulders).

Deadlift

The deadlift is simply how to pick up heavy objects off the floor with good form. It builds great grip strength, strong legs and a strong back. There are a few variations to the deadlift and some if done incorrectly will affect the lower back. Heavy deadlifts are best kept out of the training program or just in the pre-season training for the OCR athlete. Remember that a deadlift is not a squat, the hips do not go up and down. The hips go back and forwards. Work with a strength coach in person to help get the correct form for you.

Kettlebell/Dumbbell Deadlift
- Place KB/DB in between feet. Feet will be about shoulder width apart. If using a DB, place the DB vertically on the ground on its side so it looks like a column.
- Grab KB/DB by the handle/end of DB
- Push hips back until your shins are vertical and straighten back.
- Press feet into the ground and stand up, squeezing your glutes

Suitcase Deadlift

Single KB/DB

This version requires good bracing of the shoulder joint and core in order for them to remain stable. You are fighting to stay upright and not be pulled to the side by the weight of the bell as you stand up.

The KB/DB will be outside the feet to one side.

The form is the same as above.

Double KB/DB

This is a 2 handed version with a KB/DB in each hand.

The KB/DB will be outside the feet and come up the sides of the body when you stand.

The form is the same as above.

Barbell/Sandbag Deadlift

The deadlift is sometimes called the conventional deadlift to distinguish it from other variations.

- The barbell will start on the ground with plates on the bar. If done with an empty barbell (no plates) you will stand all the way up to start.

- Stand close to the barbell with your feet underneath the bar between hip and shoulder width apart.
- Place hands on the barbell just outside your legs shoulder width apart. Knuckles will be facing away from your body when you grab the barbell. Sometimes you may see others utilizing a switch grip (sometimes called a mixed grip) which is one hand facing forward and the other backward. This is used to reduce the need for a strong grip. If utilizing this grip, you should alternate hand positions every 1-3 reps
- Sit your hips down lower than your shoulders, straighten out your back (straight spine) and pull your knees back so your shins are vertical. You should feel tightness in your hamstrings.
- The arms stay straight. Tighten the shoulder back but do not tighten the biceps
- Press the feet into the ground, start lifting the bar off the ground slowly, keep the shoulders and hips rising at the same rate until the bar gets above the knees. Then squeeze the glutes and stand up tall with the shoulders behind the barbell.
- To descend start by pushing the hips back first, keep the back straight as you lower the bar down. Keep the shins vertical (if you bend the knees forward, they will be in the way of the bar).
- Set the bar down.

Rack Pulls

Rack pulls are a great variation of the deadlift that can reduce the amount of stress placed on the lower back during the deadlift by shortening the distance lifting. You can still get some heavy weight on the bar and work the posterior chain.

In a rack pull the bar is raised off the ground in a squat rack or on a platform or boxes. The height is usually between the knees and just below the hips. This height is dependent on how much range of motion you want to work on in the lift.

Everything else in the lift is the same as the conventional deadlift except the starting height of the bar.

Sumo Deadlift

The Sumo version is wider than the hips stance. The hands are placed inside the legs and the chest is more upright than folded over. This version also removes some of the low back strain that the deadlift can produce while still allowing you to lift a good deal of weight and get stronger.

Trap Bar Deadlift

The trap bar is a hexagonal specialty bar that allows you to remove the lower back strain from deadlifting. This is set up like the double KB suitcase deadlift but allows a much greater range in loading weight due to using weight plates as loading.

This is a great alternative deadlift for anyone with back issues in the conventional deadlift. This is due to the handles being on the side and the loading of the weight being more centered vs being in front of the body.

Power Clean

The power clean and variants of it are an excellent way to develop explosive power and strength. It is a more dynamic and athletic way to get heavy objects from the ground to the shoulders. In a race this could be a heavy log or sandbag or even the heavy D-Ball that is in some stadium races. In the Power clean the idea is to move an object from the ground to your shoulders in one explosive movement. This can be accomplished multiple ways.

Barbell Power Clean

The Barbell Power Clean and Hang Power Clean are staples of most athletic performance programs. The Barbell allows you to progressively load the weight and drop the barbell (if you have rubber bumper plates on) should you fail a rep.

For Obstacle Course Racing this can be a great move that helps develop leg strength, coordination and power. It can also develop strain and tightness in the forearms and grip. Should you feel any issues with your wrists or around the elbow area it can lead to hanging and climbing issues.

The Power Clean starts with the plates on the ground and the Hang power clean starts off the ground usually just above the knee. Then using an explosive jump movement and arm pull you get the barbell to the shoulders and catch the barbell in the front rack position. The barbell is resting on the shoulders and the elbows are pointing away from your body.

Sandbag Power Clean

The sandbag variation of the power clean is a great grip and upper back development tool. I prefer this version for Obstacle racers. Some sandbags have handles or straps to grab onto while others may just be disks or bags of sand.

Dumbbell Power Clean

This dumbbell variation of the power clean can be done single handed or with both hands. This helps build great grip and pulling strength as well as core stability work.

With a dumbbell in each hand. Keep your core and back tight, push your hips back like in the deadlift and lower the DBs to either your knees (Hang) or touching the ground. Using an explosive jump movement pull the DBs up to your chest and catch them on the shoulders by pointing your elbows forward.

The DBs should come up the body in a straight line, not away from the body in an arch like a bicep curl. Stand tall to finish the movement.

Lunges

Lunges are a staple for any OCR athlete. You just cannot get around the benefit that this movement gives you for trail running and hill climbing. All lunge variations can be done just bodyweight or by adding external weight such as KB/DBs, barbells, sandbags, and weight vests.

Walking Lunges

This version is moving forward or backward using lunges. When stepping make sure that your steps are long enough so the front leg is at 90 degrees and the heel firmly planted into the ground. Try not to push off the ball of the foot to stand up.

The shoulders should stay over the hips and the spine straight. Do your best to not lean forward.

You can include weights in different ways, weight vests, on your shoulders (front or back using barbells, only front using KB/DB), overhead (plates, barbells, KB/DB), or by your side (KB/DB)

I like to add walking lunges into the end of a workout as a finisher and work up to accumulating 100 steps.

Jumping Lunges

A jumping lunge starts in a lunge position, the athlete jumps up, switches position of the feet, lands into a lunge, repeat.

If you have knee issues, jumping is not a good option. Do your best to move the feet quickly and extend fully when jumping. Stop before full fatigue sets in or when form breaks down.

Step ups

- For the purpose of this book step ups will be a variation of the lunge. You can load this variation up just the same as a walking lunge.
- Use a box or platform that you can comfortably step onto. This is usually between 12-16" for most athletes.
- Step onto the box. Drive through your front heel to standing, step down and switch feet, repeat. The core should stay tight, squeeze your glutes on the way to standing. The shoulders should stay over the hips. Avoid leaning forward to stand on the box.
- For variations in loading, you can add a weight vest, or hold weight in your hands, at your chest or on your shoulders. OCR specific variations of step ups would include KB Front Rack step ups, sandbags, and buckets.

7

CONDITIONING, CARDIO AND GRIP WORK

Photo: B. Stumpf

In this section I am grouping a few methods together conditioning, cardio-respiratory endurance and grip strength.

What Is Conditioning?

When I talk about conditioning, I am referring to conditioning used for short intense bursts of power and speed followed by a less intense period of work or rest. Such is the way with obstacle course races. We are sustaining a lower heart rate running/jogging/walking and then a huge output of energy or concentration doing an obstacle and then back into a lower heart rate state.

The way we train is usually the way we race. Proper conditioning will allow us to elevate and then lower our heart rate and use our energy properly over an extended period (Race or training). Over time in a race or training we are developing and raising our cardiorespiratory endurance so we can perform and recover adequately and be able to train again soon after. It is important to get used to these spikes in heart rate during our training. Add in these movements with moderate distance runs to get a feel of doing an obstacle and then running again.

Grip strength refers to the strength of the hands and forearms to be able to carry a load for distance or the strength to support your body weight while hanging from an obstacle. Conditioning our hands and body to carry heavy objects long distances or to support our body weight hanging from a bar is essential to this sport.

We also need to condition our mind and body for long, slow uphill treks. Without adding in a training day to grind out long sessions going uphill your body will break down quickly on race day. To build proper conditioning I like to utilize a heart rate monitor. I try to keep it in a green or aerobic zone as much as possible going uphill.

At the beginning of a season this may only be 20 mins of elevation work before I run out of gas. Each week continue to increase the time spent going uphill until you can comfortably move uphill for 60 mins.

Add in 10 mins extra each week until you hit 60 mins. After 4 weeks your Cardiorespiratory endurance will improve, and it will start to feel easier.

Once you can do 60 mins of elevation work you can also start to add weight to your elevation climbs. Carry buckets, sandbags, weights or pull a tire behind you. Again, start easy, carry weight for the first 20 mins of your 60 min session and each week add 5-10 mins of carry/drag work to your session.

Conditioning Tools

Kettlebell Swing (RKC Hardstyle swing)

The Kettlebell Swing is a versatile move that is used to build strength, conditioning and endurance. Unfortunately, I often see it done incorrectly. It is a difficult movement to develop on your own as there are many moving parts. This is where the eyes of a trained instructor can be beneficial. I highly suggest that if you want to use kettlebell swings in your training that you get a session with a kettlebell coach.

The KBS (Kettlebell swing) is a ballistic hip hinge movement. Meaning you use your hips to move the kettlebell quickly. It is important to draw the distinction that the swing is not a squat. In a squat the center of the hips goes down and up (vertical), in the swing the center of the hips goes back and forward (horizontal). The arms are only used as a guide for the kettlebell and not for any significant power. Meaning you are not pulling on the kettlebell with your arms to make it go higher.

How to do a Kettlebell Swing

Set up with the kettlebell between your feet, take a step backwards. Set your feet about shoulder width apart. Your feet and the kettlebell should now make the points of a triangle.

- Push your hips back and lower your chest down (folding at the hips not the knees). Keep the shins vertical (little to no forward angle at the ankles/shins. Keep your lower back flat. I find it helpful to think about the position a baseball shortstop player may get in. Sitting back with hands on the knees.

- Reach for the kettlebell, this will be the start of the swing called a "hike", like a hike in American football where the center snaps the football through his legs. Tighten up your shoulders and lats, this may drag the kettlebell towards you, this is good. You are now tight and ready to move the kettlebell into the swing

- Aggressively and quickly "hike" the kettlebell between the legs near the hips or groin area. Your forearms should touch your thighs and hands between your legs.

- Be sure to keep your lower back flat here. Do not let the kettlebell pull you through your legs and make you bend your back.

- Start the up motion of the swing by standing up quickly by squeezing your glutes, move your hips forward, pressing your feet into the ground and standing up tall. Do not lean back (hips in front of shoulders), your shoulders should stop above your hips like you are "standing tall".

- The Kettlebell will now have power and momentum behind it. Let it swing up between the height of the chest and shoulders. Keep a strong grip but do not "pull" the kettlebell up with the arms. Let the kettlebell float and reverse direction. The top of the swing will resemble a "Plank" position, your abs and glutes will be tight. Breathe out sharply at the top of the swing. This will help tighten your diaphragm and abdominals and lessen any potential for low back injuries.

- On the down portion of the swing be patient. Let the arms and kettlebell swing down and then "catch" them with the hips and absorb the swing. I see too many people move their hips back too soon before the kettlebell gets to the hips. If the hips go back too soon the kettlebell will start to arc too low towards the ground and the weight will be too far away from the hips which leads to the low back straining to keep the weight of the chest and kettlebell controlled. I like to think of it like a baseball catcher catching a fast ball. The hips need to catch and absorb the energy of the kettlebell. Then we can use that energy to load up the hamstrings (like pulling the string on a bow and arrow) and then "snapping" the hips forward again to start the next swing.

Farmers Carry

The Farmer's carry is a great way to develop great grip and carry strength and has an immediate transfer over to obstacle course racing (and taking all the groceries into the house in one trip). They can be done with many different implements: Dumbbells, Kettlebells, Farmers carry handles, buckets, water jugs, Jerry cans, Trap bars, and more. Essentially anything you can pick up and walk with is fair game.

The ones we usually see in a race are water jugs, jerry cans, and logs with chain handles. But in training you will want to vary what you use from handle width to weight. From single hand carries to two hand carries. Trap bars and farmers carry handles will allow you to load up the weight to be very heavy.

It can be hard to find dumbbells and kettlebells that go over 70 lbs. sometimes. Water jugs and jerry cans loaded with water are between 50-75 lbs. You can also load them with sand or pea gravel to get a heavier weight.

The proper form to do 2 handed Farmers Carries is as follows:

- Step between the handles/weights so you are grabbing them to the outside of your legs

- Start lifting by grabbing the weight and setting up like a deadlift. Hips back, shoulders over the weights, bodyweight into your heels, low back straight and core braced.
- Stand up straight by pushing your heels into the ground. Your standing posture should be straight like an "at attention" pose. Shoulders back and spine tall and straight.
- Start by walking at a comfortable pace and get used to the movement of the weight.

One of the mistakes I often see happen is bending of the back and knees in order to jog or run with the weight. These are not called farmer's runs for a reason. This fault can also happen if the weight is too heavy for the core to hold the upper body up in a good position. Identify where the form breakdown happens. Is it the weight used, or distance moved? The great thing about this exercise is that you can put it down and rest and pick it back up when you are ready to keep moving.

I personally like to use kettlebells for my carries as they are easy to move with, have thick handles, and the weight is distributed below the hand so it doesn't create any torque in the wrist if you are moving fast like some DBs or Farmers carry handles can because the weight is distributed laterally away from the grip.

Start adding these into training as short distance carries, first with moderate weight to get used to the demands on the grip then progressively going up in weight each session. A starting distance of 4-5 rds. of 20m (80-100m total) should be good to start with and may seem a bit easy at first. You can increase the weight or the distance if you become comfortable with either. The shorter distances are good to help build the grip strength needed to start working on longer carries.

To test yourself, you can try to do a max distance carry. Have the distance measured out before you start. Choose a moderate weight and see how far you can walk before having to put it down. Most obstacle course races will have a heavy carry between 200-400m long. Get used to the long carry.

Sled Push/Pull

The sled push is one of the great ways to build leg pushing strength, core strength, and build a great base of cardio. It can be used for short, fast interval sprints (running) but also heavier, more grueling pushes (walking or lunges).

If you live in a flat area without hills, sled pushes are a great alternative to hill work. Work up to being able to push your bodyweight (sled weight + extra plates) on the sled. Alternate the pushes with pulling the sled every few weeks or even in the same session. This can be forward or backward walking/sprinting. To accomplish this, you will need a rope and belt/harness to pull the sled.

A non-gym option is the tire drag. Get an old car or truck tire, attach a length of rope to the tire and the other end to your waist and start walking. If you want to jog or sprint with the tire, first make sure that it is heavy enough to not start bouncing around behind you.

Hill Sprints

Photo: R. Borgatti

For obstacle course racing, hill sprints are necessary. Hill sprints, whether short or long, should be an integral part of your training program. I like to have them included once a week or every other week depending on how much lower body lifting an athlete is doing. These do require a good warm up and should not be started cold.

Do your sprints on various surfaces if possible, such as a street, trail, grass and fire road/packed road version that you can alternate each week. It's okay if you cannot go all out up a hill at first. Try to increase the distance you can go each week without stopping. Walk back to the start and rest almost double the time it took you to sprint up. Each week reduce the rest if possible.

Start off with easy distances and elevation gains 4x 100-200m in distance and 50-100m in elevation gain, start slow and make the last one the fastest.

Over time find a hill that is 300-400m long with 150-200m of elevation gain and work on a moderate but constant pace up the hill. Increase speed gradually over 4-6 weeks.

Fan Bike

The fan bike is a great tool to work on conditioning. This bike can really allow you to push to the edge of your comfort zone. Most beginners shy away from using the Fan Bike because it can make you feel uncomfortable.

Start by using it in warmups, about 5 mins at a comfortable pace. After a few weeks you should be comfortable enough to add it into workouts. Start with timed intervals like 1 minute on/off the bike at a moderate pace. The shorter the time the more intense the work should be. Most athletes cannot push hard for more than :20s when they first use the bike.

These Fan bikes are showing up in more stadium and urban style races where you must complete a specific number of calories at the station. I like to pair intense, short intervals on the bike with different types of carries or spear throws. It is a great way to work on grip or accuracy with a high heart rate.

8

RUNNING

Photo: D. Fatula, Athlete: R. Borgatti

At the heart of all Obstacle Course races is running. Even though you can walk on the course, running is an integral part of the experience. Whether it is a stadium race, going up and down stairs, to a mountain resort covering thousands of feet of elevation, running will get you to the finish line (and medal) faster. The primary terrain of these races is dirt trails, fire roads and single-track switchbacks. So, training and understanding trail running is a must to get the whole challenge.

Trail running is full of small obstacles and details that road runners do not have to regularly deal with. There are lots of roots and rocks and changes of terrain. The height changes, the angles change and the surface changes. It can be soft and mossy one minute and then slick and rocky the next.

Concentration is key when trail running. You cannot "turn off" and run in the woods. You must be present and aware of the ground and where your next step will be.

Over the years of trail running, I have noticed that anytime my mind has drifted and lost focus that is the moment I injure myself. Perhaps I was thinking about what happened in my day or something that I am doing later, or just daydreaming. I realized too late that I stopped looking at the trail and making micro adjustments to my running.

I have learned this lesson the hard way with quite a few broken toes and sprained ankles to remind me to stay present and engaged on the trail.

New to Running

If you are just beginning to run, I have included below some of the major issues or questions that may come up as well as some answers. Running is a high impact activity. In the beginning you will essentially be doing strength training as you are imparting 1.5x your bodyweight in forces on each leg as you run. As you get more conditioned and stronger it will become easier.

How to start running

Most beginner runners do not stick with running due to a few issues. Most are just the wrong way to start out and some can be psychological or based on past performance. If an athlete who has had preconceived notions about running from the past (I am not a runner) starting slower and shorter could help lead them to a love of running.

Perceived difficulty

If it feels hard, slow it down, reduce the distance or do both. There is nothing that says you need to suffer or go harder than you can handle. Start with walking or a pace that is comfortable. Set a time goal rather than a distance goal. Like just move for 20 mins. Time on your feet and consistency is more important. This is probably the hardest for most younger or former athletes as we "remember" going faster. Many non-runners start by going way too hard at the beginning, perhaps thinking they must make up for lost time. Even if it's shuffling your feet and running at a pace most walk at, keep going. If you can talk and move, you are doing great!

Wrong pace/heart rate level

I like to wear a watch with a heart rate monitor or chest strap while running. Different running conditions or even your mental state can push you out of the correct HR zone for your run. A sprint workout should not have a low heart rate and a long slow run should not have a high heart rate. Sometimes on my long slow runs the humidity can be so high that even though I am not going fast my heart rate starts to get too high, so I need to slow down. Gathering data and evaluating it over time can really help you set safe boundaries for running. Especially if you are over 35, as we get older our heart rate zones could change especially if we took time off running or doing aerobics work.

Too hard, too fast

There are a few reasons for an athlete to push the pace too much. The first is the athlete just does not know their training pace or objective for that distance (not prepared or planned, just went out running), they used to run at that pace, but they are older or injured (ego). This is usually the main cause for beginner athletes to quit running

Something hurts

This is usually a nagging injury that is not being taken care of or little to no warmup protocol. The harder and faster you are planning on running the more involved the warmup should be. Take your time warming up nagging areas, use tools like foam rollers and lacrosse balls to perform SMR on the area.

Hydration plays a big role on how joints and muscles feel. Make sure you are getting an adequate amount of water and electrolytes 48 hours before longer runs

The best method to start running I have found is to walk/run for a set amount of time or distance. First start with a time frame (I will move for 15 mins) and increase that time by 5 mins each week for 4-6 weeks. Such as week 1: 15 mins, week 2: 20 mins, etc. until 45 mins. Record the distance moved for that time such as "I ran/jogged 1 mile in 15 mins, walked 3 times".

If you are unable to complete that week's running, go back to the previous weeks' time for 2 weeks, then if successful, go back up. Continue until you can move for 45 mins without stopping to walk, it can still be a jog.

Road Running vs Trail Running

If you are used to road running, a trail run, or race can be a different beast. Trail running requires a bit of flexibility and strength that is not always needed on the road. You must be able to pick your feet and knees to get over rocks and roots. Often there are much more rolling hills which will require you to power up causing you to switch between aerobic and anaerobic work. Jumping and landing properly may be needed going over streams, rocks, and roots.

Getting lost in the woods does sometimes happen. Keep your phone with you to find your way out or back to a trail. Luckily these days phones have GPS and unlimited data. There are many apps with trail maps available as well. Newer smart training watches now also have trail map data available.

If you have some road running times and places you can easily estimate your trail running pace. Just Add 2-3 mins to your road pace (time per mile) to find your trail pace. Your speed and pace per mile will change drastically from mile to mile. In the same 6-mile loop that I do I sometimes have a 7 min pace right next to a 12 min pace due to the terrain.

Get used to uneven terrain

Running on uneven and ever-changing terrain takes practice and a change in running form from the road. Your gait and foot speed will need to be adjusted. Use shorter but slightly higher steps on the trails. Stay light on your feet. Choose your running line a few feet ahead and pay attention to any obstructions. You will naturally drift from side to side on the trail trying to avoid a bad running path.

In the gym you can work on agility ladder drills to help improve your lateral awareness and weight distribution. If you know your average steps per min on your runs, try and use that as a starting speed for the agility drills then ramp up the foot speed. Work on your lateral movement drills in your warmups. Trail running requires some quick lateral movements to avoid obstacles.

Running in an OCR

An Obstacle Course race can be fun for people who do not like to run a lot. It is not like a road race where you are constantly moving. Most obstacles in a race are no longer than 1-2 miles apart so it offers plenty of opportunities to stop and rest between bouts of running.

Most people just need to run 1-3 miles continuously and then get a break while they complete an obstacle and wait for teammates. Most of the terrain can be difficult so it lends itself to a bit slower running naturally as well.

If you do like to run, an OCR can challenge your ability to switch between anaerobic and aerobic capacities. The starting and stopping can bring out some weak points in an excellent road runner. But once those weak spots are taken care of, a good runner will start to pull away from the pack.

Most Terrain in an OCR is on single track trails or fire roads. Only a small percentage of races take place on road or concrete. Trail running requires good body awareness and reaction time. Trail running works on some different muscles than road running. Strong hamstrings and glutes are needed for up and down hill running. Full range of motion for the hips are important for injury prevention. Calves seem to be the muscle group that cramps the fastest and most often which I attribute to being under trained for the terrain.

Elevation and Mountain Running

Running Uphill

Uphill running is probably the most taxing of movements in an OCR and only the competitive or elite need to be very good at this. Most of us just need to be conditioned enough to keep moving. The uphill's can be anywhere from a 5 -10 degree up to a max of a major 20-to-30-degree incline. That is almost crawling uphill at that angle, which was the case for some parts of the 2014 Spartan Championship Beast at Killington Mountain. And some parts of the downhill of the 2017 Killington Beast where even the elite athletes were sliding on their backsides down the hill.

Fast hiking is better than running the longer the race is. This will help keep your heart rate down and conserve some energy. The less you must stop to rest the faster you will be overall. Consider sprinting 100m, uphill. You would max out your heart rate and it may take up to 2-3 minutes to recover to do it again. This is also an anabolic movement which is the wrong engine we want to use. We want to keep this Aerobic (Cardiorespiratory) keeping our body moving at a moderate heart rate at a sustainable pace. If you do need to stop it would only take 30-60 seconds to recover to start moving again. It's the old story of the tortoise and the hare. Slow and steady wins the race. Especially if it's uphill for long distances.

Shorter distances such as a Spartan sprint or 5k race there is no time to stop and walk if you are trying to race. There is simply no room to make up the time. Your running/fast hiking helps give you time in case you miss an obstacle that has penalties. Uphill movements require a good degree of ankle flexion as well. Good ankle flexion will allow you to lean into the climb and not cause any calf or tendon issues.

Good core strength will keep your torso upright. If you collapse at your midsection, you are moving your center of gravity forward which will make you feel heavier due to some inefficient movement.

Try not to look at your feet. Pick a spot about 30m away and stay fixed on that spot and keep moving towards it. When you get there, picture a new target to move towards. This will keep you mentally engaged on your task and not overwhelmed by the entire length of the climb. Small, Achievable goals will keep you motivated.

Downhill Running

Running downhill can be more taxing in some cases. To go downhill you need great ankle extension and strong quads. Lots of racers let the downhill slow them down too much. They put on the breaks due to fear, uncertainty, lack of training and exposure to the angle of the slope. If you put on the brakes too much the knees start to hurt, muscles start to cramp, and this becomes more of a strength movement trying to slow your descent and stay in control.

Start practicing downhill runs on small, short hills. Get comfortable feeling the pull of gravity and finding a good medium between falling and fully stopping your momentum. Let the hips stay loose and turn over your feet quickly but using short steps. Avoid leaning back too much as this will cause you to start sliding down the hill or have your feet push out in front of you causing you to fall backwards.

A natural way to slow down while going downhill has been utilized by downhill recreational skiers forever. The traverse. Go down in 45-degree angles moving side to side on the trail. Use your legs to absorb the impact by keeping them slightly bent. Be careful of loose gravel or dirt when doing this. You will naturally lean into the hillside a bit.

Getting better at going up hills

If you feel that you slow down to almost a crawl when going up hills or feel like you just cannot go fast up a hill, then you need to incorporate 1-2x weeks of hill training. A shorter hill sprint and a longer sustained run up a long hill. Start first by fast walking the hills and jogging down. After a few weeks, switch to run/walk up the hills and jog down. And finally work on a sustained run effort up the entire hill. I outline some tips for each next.

Getting better at downhill running

Start with a small hill and get comfortable leaning into the run and not holding back. Most runners lean away from the hill and put on the brakes. Learn to let your feet turn over quickly and use your legs to absorb your body weight as you go down the hill. Do this as a circuit 6-8x where you walk up the hill and jog/run down the hill.

For steep hills practice traversing (going side to side) down the trail/ hill. Learning what speed feels good for taking corners and what your body will handle will take some practice. Also pay attention to the different terrain. Traversing on dry dirt, mud, rocks and sand all require different speeds and foot placement so you do not slip and fall.

Short Hill Sessions

Do these like a circuit. 4-6x up a hill as fast and as far as you can go. Note how far you made it. Set a marker about 30m before you run out of gas. Work on moving quickly from the base of the hill to the marker. When you can make all 6 sets then move the marker farther away (10m) for the next session.

Long Hill Sessions

Add longer hill run training to your schedule 1-2x a week. Longer hill runs should be at a moderate pace that you can sustain for the full distance. Set a baseline by choosing a hill that is challenging but not too hard or technical. Jog up the hill at a pace you can hold. Note time/distance. If you feel you have to recover and you have to catch your breath at the top of the hill, then you may have been going too fast.

When you can comfortably make the run to the top (this may take 4-5 weeks) start working on getting faster and recovering faster. I do not believe that it is how fast you can make it up the hill but how smart you can be about keeping moving and not gassing out towards the top as well as who can recover and keep going after the ascent.

What if I don't live near a mountain?

The best way to train for a steep grade without having access to one is twofold:

Gain access to a treadmill with the steepest incline you can find, start with the Incline treadmill test In the OCR Fitness Benchmark section. There are only a few models of treadmills on the market that have a very steep setting to simulate extreme hill climbs (20-30 degrees), but any treadmill at max incline will do. You can also add a weight vest, dumbbell carries or a sandbag to add resistance to the walk/jog on the treadmill

If you have access to a sled start by doing slow and fast sled pushes. The slow sled push should be more like fast walking/hiking than sprinting. Start light and add weight and distance each week. If you are doing a race like the Spartan Beast Build up to the challenge of a 1600m (1M) sled push with half to full BW added onto the sled.

Building Endurance

In order to work on endurance correctly we must know what is meant by endurance. How do we define endurance? Is running the only way to build endurance? One definition state: "the fact or power of enduring an unpleasant or difficult process or situation without giving way". We could say that building endurance is increasing our ability to keep going under challenging circumstances, such as a long race or harsh conditions.

This could be increasing distances such as in running or rowing, Increasing the difficulty such as uphill walking or running. Making normally easy tasks more challenging by adding increased time or load like we would see in rucking or adding bodyweight movements to the task (running and burpees).

Increasing or building endurance takes incremental work utilizing long steady distance training. This may look like adding a half a mile (800m) to each long run or adding 250m to a long row distance for 6 weeks. An example template may look like this each week:

Running:

Week 1: 1 Mile

Week 2: 1.5 Miles

Week 3: 2 Miles

Week 4: 2.5 Miles

Week 5: 3 Miles

Week 6: 3.5 Miles

You could also do it by adding time to your runs but not a specific distance. We call this "Time on your feet". This is a great option for beginner runners as there is no expectation of distance. It is a good idea to note how far you went in the allotted time. If a race is estimated to take 3 hours, we should work up to being able to move for that long regardless of the distance we travel. When doing this method, it is best to stick to the same course.

This method of building endurance may look like this:

Running:

Week 1: Run/walk 20 mins

Week 2: Run/walk 25 mins

Week 3: Run/walk 30 mins

Week 4: Run/walk 35 mins

Week 5: Run/walk 40 mins

Week 6: Run/walk 45 mins

These two methods can be applied to any aerobic movement like rowing, hiking or biking. Building endurance is all about time moving at an aerobic pace. You can work on it through multiple methods to keep any overuse injuries and boredom.

We also want to avoid adding in extra weekly distance for no reason. In running circles these are called "Junk Miles". Junk miles increase the chances of developing overuse injuries.

Training Runs for OCR

Training runs for an OCR should be broken up between trail and other running. Trails can be fire roads or hiking trails. Other running can be road, treadmill, hills or sprints. Here is a hypothetical breakdown of running ratios. 60% trail and 40% other running.

The 60% trail work can be split up into even parts 20% short and fast, 20% moderate distance runs with tempo/elevation, and 20% long and slow.

The 40% other running can be split up into 15% road or treadmill work, 15% hill work, and 10% sprint work.

The distances you will run on these training runs will depend on the races you are training for and your schedule. A 5k run plan will look different than a ½ marathon plan as would a race with a 900 ft elevation vs a 4000 ft elevation. The shorter and flatter the race the more speed work should be done versus a mountain race where time getting conditioned to elevation gain is crucial.

If you are just starting your first few weeks may consist of a lot of walking and that is okay! If you do not meet your goal during a training run, adjust the distances a bit for the next few runs. One of the worst things you can do is miss a few runs and then try to jump back in at a higher distance or pace.

If you feel that you are a slow runner then speed work and track days may be beneficial. This is not as important for a beginner runner as it is for someone who may be experienced at running but feels slow. Start off easy with adding in a few Fartlek Runs to start. Just pick some times during your moderate distance run to alternate between going fast and slow

A typical 3x week run schedule may look something like this:
- Day 1: Interval Track work or hill sprints
- Example 4x400m
- Day 2: Tempo Run
- Example 3M road run, 1st mile slow, 2nd mile fast, 3rd mile slow
- Day 3: Long slow run
- Example 6M trail run, slow pace

Below I outline some training pointers and advice for training runs for each of the distances. This is more to illustrate the differences in training runs, schedules and priorities so you can develop a running program that fits your needs. As with all things, find what fits you best. If speed work or tempo runs do not feel right to you it's okay to adjust the plan.

Urban/Stadium Short races

Training to be competitive for a short race can be one of the hardest things an athlete can do. Progress can be tracked in seconds rather than minutes. Most of the urban/stadium races are short and fast paced. For this I suggest lots of mid distance speed work and stadium climbs. Be careful to take your time to properly warm up before working on speed work. Be able to keep moving for 45 – 60 mins

Training plans for short stadium races should include:

- Running stadium stairs
- Short to mid distance speed 200m, 400m, and 800m sprints
- Include 10 burpees after all runs
- Agility and cone work.
- Long runs of 2-3M

Most stadiums have tight areas between chairs and tight turns around corners. Work on footwork and cone drills to keep the feet quick and work on your lateral starting, stopping and changing directions.

5K Races

Training runs for 5K races will be a mix of road or treadmill and trail runs. These races can be a lot of start and stop with a few long stretches of running. We start to see mild elevation and some single tracks on the course. Be able to keep moving for 60 - 90 mins

Training plans for 5K races should include:

- 1x week hill work
- Developing a good uphill sprint that you can recover quickly from
- Mid distance speed work 400m, 800m and 1600m
- 1x week Tempo run work of 2-5M
- Train in all kinds of weather
- Include 10-20 burpees every mile on trail runs
- Long Runs of 3-5M

- Carry objects (sandbag, stones, logs, etc.) for portions of the long run (200-400m)

10K Races

Training for a 10k distance race will make most beginners uncomfortable at first. Work on getting your running up to a comfortable pace or just being used to being on your feet for 90 -120 mins.

Training plans for 5K races should include:

- 1x week hill/interval work
- 1x week Tempo work of 3-6M
- Long Runs up to 7-10M miles.
- Start adding in carries and body weight movements before, during and/or after the runs.

Running Volume and Tapering

Weekly Running Volume

Running volume and distances are based on the race you are training for. It's no secret that someone training for a marathon will run more than someone training for a 5k. The shorter a race the more speed work and tempo runs you may want to do. The longer a race the more time you will spend out on longer, slower paced runs. Higher volume can be beneficial for aerobic capacity but does increase the risk of injury.

Too much speed work can also cause injuries such as hamstring strains or tears. Most of your training will be in the middle of the two. Your longest run will come within 75-105% of the race distance. It is not always needed to run longer than your race distance. Some athletes feel they need to run longer than the race distance to help build confidence that they can complete the race. The conditioning and quality of the runs are the most important.

In obstacle course racing you will be switching between aerobic and anaerobic activities. It is important to add anaerobic activities to your runs such as burpees, pushups, pull ups, squats, heavy carries, etc. This will help build your capacity to not only run the distance but be able to perform strength tasks.

In a 10k (6.2 M) race training the weekly volume will peak at 14-16M for the week with the longest run being 6-8M. This is less weekly mileage than some training programs. The training distance is slightly longer than a 10k road race because the OCR distances do not count the obstacle distances such as the heavy carries. So, in an OCR you are usually travelling/running farther than the posted race distance. Be prepared when the race mileage and your watch do not match

Tapering

Tapering is typically a lower or little to no volume training leading up to the race. This can start as early as 2-3 weeks before the race date. This is meant to dial back the volume, give you a chance to rest and recover from training and set you up to perform your best on race day. Some athletes can do well with less activity during this time while other athletes cannot stand the idleness and lack of movement.

This can be a very mentally difficult time for an athlete as they feel like they are not doing enough to prepare for the race. I believe that you should move a bit the day or 2 days before a race. Too many athletes say they feel sluggish or un-trained the day of the race when they take off the day or two right before the race. These easy sessions should be just enough to keep mentally healthy and not strenuous at all.

For athletes that have trouble resting here is a good, suggested plan for tapering using running volume percentages:

Follow the 80/60/30 prescription. For an example I will use the numbers from the 10k training program later in the book. The highest volume week is 14M in a week. This training tapering strategy can work for any race distance:

- 3 weeks before race, lower total running volume down to 80%

- (Ex: 11M: 1,4,6M runs)
- 2 weeks before race, lower total weekly volume down to 60% (8M)
- 1 week before race, lower total weekly running volume down to 30% (4M)

This is also true for any cross training that an athlete may be doing leading up to a race. As an athlete lowers the running and resistance training volume they should add in some extra time for mobility and light stretching.

Gait and Cadence

What is Gait and Cadence?

Gait is simply the way or process of how we walk. Sometimes called the gait cycle. It is the biomechanical way we walk, our footfalls, our pronation of the feet, and where we land on the foot when we walk or run.

Gait analysis is the process by which you are videoed walking or running and are assessed on how your foot strikes the ground (forefoot, midfoot, or heel) Also if your foot fall is neutral, over pronates, or under pronates when it lands. Gait analysis can also show you mechanical issues or compensations happening in the knees, hips, or torso that may lead to issues or injuries in the future.

Cadence is how many steps we take per minute (SPM). This is also called stride rate. A few things affect our cadence when we run: stride length, our foot landing, and speed. The shorter your stride length, the faster your cadence. The more efficient your stride or gait, the easier it is to turn over your footfalls. This is what we want while running so we land on the mid foot and not over stride and heel strike.

Most beginner and intermediate runners overstride when they run. This leads to inefficient movement and heel striking when landing. This can also, over time, lead to running injuries such as knee, hip or foot issues.

To help correct this we can use a metronome device or app that will help us speed up our footfalls which will shorten our stride. We can also use form drills to help us repattern the way we run. I highly suggest finding a running coach who knows how to do these footwork drills and is experienced interpreting running video.

Using A Metronome for Cadence

Use a metronome or running app that counts steps per minute. Most apps allow you to beep to both footfalls or just one footfall (L or R). For beginners it is easier to set it to the beep happening on just their dominant side.

Start by finding a comfortable cadence that you can hold for a minute. Some athletes may find that 60 BPM (120 steps/min) is too slow. Your starting cadence will be between 70 and 80 BPM (140-160 steps per min).

Work on increasing it to as close to 90 BPM (180 steps per min) that you can sustain for 1 lap or 1 min.

Run Distance Strategies

I have included some specific running programs in the appendix. Please refer to them to get a better idea on how to get faster or better at running these distances. Running is a skill and like any skill to get better you must practice and train that skill. Read through the next chapter on Race classifications to get some idea on what each type of race will need for training.

9

TRAINING STRATEGY FOR OBSTACLE COURSE RACES

Photo: P. Bernardi

Obstacle Course Races come in a variety of challenges and distances. From short Olympic distance races to long endurance and mentally challenging races like the Spartan Ultra and Death Race. Below I will sum up each distance of race and the types of obstacles in each and offer training tips for each. These can be used for a reference when training for races of different types in a single season.

Urban/Olympic/Stadium races

- Distance: 1.5-2.5M,
- Avg time to complete: 40-60 mins

Photo: Spartan Media Team

About this race:

Stadium and Urban style OCRs have become very popular in large cities. These races are usually under 5K/3M long and sometimes take place in an iconic setting such as Fenway Park, Citi Field or similar sports stadiums. Sometimes they can be held in a large field or urban venue.

These races are great for beginners to start with. As a coach this is the type of race, I point my new clients towards conquering first. Especially if running may be an issue or if they have a limitation that being lost in the woods would be bad.

These urban races are doable with minimal training time (4-6 weeks). The races are short distances and have lots of fun obstacles. This makes it ideal for a team of friends to support each other, go at the same pace and have fun. The Fun factor is really important to a first-time racer. It will be a challenge but one that will generate fun stories and strong bonds.

Common Obstacles

- **Stairs**

Lots and lots of stairs! These races do not have a lot of running room, so they get creative on creating distance. That involves going up and down stairs and concourses. In your training make sure you are adding in a day of going up and down stairs. Doesn't matter if it is walk, jog or run but you will need to work up to 30-40 mins of specific stairs or incline work to condition your quads and calves to the constant up and down.

- **Functional Gym Movements**

These races make up for the lack of big obstacles with lots of exercises found in Functional Gyms. These should be familiar to most gym goers and may include the following:

- **Jump rope**

The races usually have a thick rope (1") that is hard to jump with. The jump pattern is a bit different than a regular gym jump rope.

- **Slam Ball**

A 20-to-30-pound ball that does not bounce. You will need to lift it over your head and "slam" it back to the ground.

- **Burpees**

We all know, and love burpees (Right?) get down to the ground, stand up, jump. Expect to do between 20 - 60 in a race so add them into your training. In some styles of urban races, you may be doing burpees holding an implement such as a weight or ball. Take your time with these if they are an obstacle and not a penalty. They will increase your heart rate quickly.

- **Climbing Obstacles**

   Rope climb, Wall climbs and an A-Frame climb. Expect Just one rope approximately 12-15' off the ground. 4-8 climbing walls ranging from 4', 6 and 8' at various points of the race.

- **Heavy carries**

   Water jugs from 30-50# that you hold or use as a Farmer's carry can be found at these races. Sometimes they will use anything with a handle or gym style equipment that can be carried.

- **Sandbags**

   One or two 30-50# sandbags that you carry up and down stairs. Sometimes twice in a race. These are a challenge for most people, so it is a great idea to add them into your training often.

- **Terrain**

   These races are in urban environments so that means lots of concrete, stairs and sometimes turf! No special gear is typically required for this terrain. Normal gym shoes and attire will suffice. Outer layers may be dependent on the time of year and weather as some portions may be outside. Take your time going around corners or objects like chairs. Most people that get injured at these style races just misjudged a turn or hit their leg into an object during a turn.

- **Training Tips**

   Unless you are in a competitive heat, I suggest that you go at a pace that's comfortable for you. Walk/jog/run upstairs in training to get used to the constant up/down. There is not a lot of distance or elevation within a stadium but trust that the race designers will find a way for you to go up and down flights of stairs as many times as they can. Lunges will help strengthen your legs for those stairs. Most carries such as sandbags or object carries will be up and down stairs as well. Put these often in your training.

They try to cram lots of obstacles into a small space so there will not be a lot of downtime between obstacles so train your ability to switch between different obstacles like a military short course may have. (Ex: wall climb to rope climb to traverse wall to hoist to monkey bars all within a few feet of each other)

CrossFit style workouts are great training for this style of races. They often include lots of the same or similar movements and can be in the same time domain (45-60 mins).

- **Training Time**

Training for this race can be anywhere from 2 - 6 weeks depending on your current fitness level and regimen. Not much time is needed to prepare for a stadium type sprint for the recreational obstacle runner. Due to the relatively easy terrain a person could technically walk the entire course.

At a minimum athletes should be able to:

- Walk/jog 5K
- Be used to moving for 45-60 mins
- Be able to climb a wall with a team
- Be able to climb a rope
- Carry heavy objects: 25 gal. water jug, 30-50# sandbag

- **Coaches Notes**

Make this a fun event for your athletes. Take pictures! Run with your team. If you want to compete or want to support a competitive athlete that's great, competitive athletes race earlier so schedule your team to race a bit later or on a different day. Race or support your athlete then go back and run with your team.

Short Races

- Distance: 3-5M/5-7k.
- Avg time to complete: 45-90 mins

Photo: A. Fatula

About this race:

Short trail races are another great starting race. These races can be typically described as fun mud runs. You will most likely get wet and dirty but will not be out on the course for too long.

An example of a short race would be the Spartan Sprint. Which is 3.5-5M long with 15-20 obstacles

Elites usually finish in 35 - 45 mins, most noncompetitive athletes finish in 1 - 1.5 hours

If conditions are good, you will not need a hydration pack or nutrition during the race unless the weather is extreme such as 90+ degrees or really high humidity.

These short races are a good mix of short runs and strength/agility obstacles. Typically, you can expect an average of 400m between obstacles that are not bunched together. The terrain will start to play a big part in the pacing of the athlete over a stadium type race. If you are trying to race the course you will need the ability to travel up hills quickly and through water hazards.

With more room outside, designers can get creative with the obstacles such as jumping over hay bales, tire flips, mud crawls, log carries and similar obstacles.

For beginners I suggest a hydration bottle or pack to run with if it is your first obstacle race. Most athletes will not need extra nutrition on the course.

Common Obstacles

- **Mud**

These races are usually a mix of trail and mud. In the earlier days of OCR these would be called fun mud runs. Traction does become an issue and I highly suggest a good trail running shoe.

- **Crawls**

From mud crawls under barbed wire to crawling through tubes or in water there will be a portion of the race where you need to crawl. Be sure you are comfortable getting down on all fours and crawling.

- **Climbs/Walls**

From walls to ropes expect to see a handful of climbing obstacles. These may include a 10-15' rope climb, 4' and 6' walls or wall-like obstacles, 10' cargo nets, slip walls, and inverted walls or structures. Bad weather can make any of these a challenge even for experienced racers. If you are not running in an elite heat, then teamwork will be a good option to conquer these climbing obstacles. It is okay to give it your best attempt and then move on if needed. Some will have a penalty depending on the style of race.

- **Heavy carries**

Most new racers have never done these types of carries in this environment. Dragging stones through mud, carrying logs uphill, or buckets filled with gravel. These can be tedious and challenging obstacles for the uninitiated. Understand that these carries slow you down and take some time to accomplish.

- **Terrain**

Terrain is flat to rugged, sometimes mountainous but usually low elevation.

The terrain will be dependent on the geographical location and weather conditions. The course creators do try to create some single-track trails through some challenging terrain. Trying to move too fast over unstable or muddy areas can be challenging.

- **Training Tips**
  - Be able to trail run 5k to 7k
  - Condition the calves and quads for uphill hiking/running
  - Train carrying heavy objects (Buckets, sandbags, dumbbells/kettlebells) for up to 400m
  - Train your grip strength by doing farmers carries and deadlifts
  - Practice running before/after obstacles, transitioning is often where people slow down
  - Work on your core strength every day from different angles if possible
  - Due to the body being put into some odd positions during races, work on flexibility and mobility before and after each training session. Pay attention to the hamstrings, calves, and shoulders

- **Training Time**

4-6 weeks

More time and conditioning are needed for a beginner for this race. Athletes will need to be able to trail run 3-5M. This can be a walk run style, but you shouldn't be wiped out by it so pace appropriately.

- **Coaches Notes**

Make sure athletes' aerobic capacity gets built up appropriately. If they are too deconditioned it will become too much of a mental grind to get through the course. Fatigue on obstacles is a quick way to an injury. Keep athletes aware of their fatigue levels and how to make good choices when tired. Let them know it's okay to rest before tackling an obstacle

Medium Races

- Distance: 7-10M/13-15k
- Avg Time to complete: 2-3hrs

Photo: CMC Media Team

About this race:

A good example of this distance race would be the Spartan Super. Which is 10K long with 15-20+ obstacles throughout.

Competitive Athletes can usually finish in 1-1.5hrs, most athletes can finish in 2-3.5 hours depending on pacing and weather conditions and elevation of the course.

If conditions are good, you may not need a hydration pack or nutrition during the race if you are used to those distances in training. Perhaps just a running water bottle. If it's hot, I suggest taking a hydration pack.

Newer racers may need food at the 4–5-mile mark or directly after finishing the course. These distances are just long enough to start to require some good mental conditioning, and nutrition planning pre-race. I find that over 6 miles I need a plan for what to eat beforehand and maybe a snack around the 4–5-mile mark to keep my energy up for the obstacles.

Common Obstacles

These have similar obstacles as the short races plus a few more challenging variations.

- **Tire Flips**

With the extra distance also comes some extra obstacles. The tire flip may be one of them. Here you get under a tire, deadlift it up and flip it over multiple times.

- **Pull/push**

Sled or tire push/pulls may be seen here. These are usually placed in mud to make it more challenging to move the weighted object through the terrain. The sled or tire is attached to a rope that you pull to you and then push back into place.

- **Extra carries**

More carries and harder terrain to carry them on. Expect to carry up hills and through woods.

- **Water**

    Welcome to getting wet! While the shorter races may have a few water obstacles the longer races will have a few that will submerge you. Sometimes under barbed wire or a section of fence in a moat.

- **Elevation**

    The longer races will tend to take place in areas that will have challenging elevation gain. Expect to travel up and down multiple times throughout the race. This can be hard on the legs so be okay conserving your energy when going uphill.

- **Terrain**

    The longer races will start to have rolling hills to mountainous terrain. This can be slightly challenging for a new racer but doable with proper pacing. The courses usually contain mud, single track trails through the woods, and uphill climbs. Expect to see water obstacles along the course as well.

- **Training Tips**
    - These races require a degree of strength endurance for grip and longer trail runs.
    - Add in heavy carries and a variety of bodyweight movements in the middle and end of long runs
    - Work on hanging obstacles that will tax your grip
    - Add running after strength workouts and obstacle work while fatigued
    - Train with your hydration pack on long runs

- **Training Time**

    6-8 weeks are needed to prepare for this race. A good aerobic base will go a long way for all racers and make the distance more enjoyable. Be able to run/jog 10k without stopping.

- **Coaches Notes**

    Most athletes will need a good running base for this distance race. It is long enough for weather to be a factor (cold in the morning and warm in the afternoon). Fatigue, Hydration, nutrition and endurance will all be tested so mental training and positive talk may be needed for the racer. Cramping is very common at this distance. This can be avoided with proper training and hydration. Due to fatigue and a lack of conditioning injuries can happen easily at this distance. Practice proper trail and obstacle transitions and awareness.

Long Races

- Distance: 12M+/20k+
- Avg time to complete: 4-8 hours

Photo: Spartan Media Team,
Athletes: R. Borgatti, L. Goulding, C. Goulding

About This Race

    A good example of this distance race would be the Spartan Beast. The Spartan Beast is 14+M through mountainous and rugged terrain with 25+ obstacles. Elites usually finish in 4-5 hours but most first timers or unprepared athletes can take up to 8-10+ hours to complete.

You must have the proper gear for a race of this distance. Night gear such as a glow stick and headlamp are a must as you most likely will not finish before sundown. If you do not have these, you may be kicked off course. You will need food and to carry your own water (hydration pack)

Weather can change drastically throughout a race this long depending on the time of year, elevation and location. I suggest packing a wind breaker or extra clothing in your pack in case of hypothermia or conditions that may cause it. There will usually be 2-3 water obstacles, weather and time of year permitting. The water obstacles may close if it becomes dangerous.

Common Obstacles

At a race of this distance expect almost all types of obstacles from shorter races to be present. There are usually a few water obstacles at races of this distance. Be prepared to possibly swim as well. If there is swimming as an obstacle, life preservers are handed out.

- **Terrain**

These races are a challenge and that includes the terrain as well expect this race to take place on a mountain or ski resort. Expect multiple ascents to the peak(s) with very steep ups and downs.

- **Training tips**

Work on lots of elevation training, get comfortable moving uphill on steep inclines. Lots of hiking and time on your feet. Build to long hikes of 3+ hours Practice long downhill runs and staying in control of your descents.

During training runs practice wearing your race gear for long periods. Chaffing can seriously be detrimental at this distance and even stop an athlete from completing.

25+ obstacles over 12+ miles can really fatigue your grip. Add in grip training and pull training into long run training sessions. Double up on some obstacles like Herc hoists and rope climbs back-to-back to build your grip.

These long races will tax your mind and resolve as well. Be okay getting uncomfortable and challenging yourself. Positive self-talk is extremely important at these distances.

- **Training Time**

    8-12 weeks at a minimum.

- **Coaches Notes**

    Make sure your athlete is prepared with lots of time on their feet moving.

    Fueling becomes important. Do not introduce anything new within 2 weeks of a long race. Stick to what has been working in training for race day. Your athlete may want to try that new, shiny energy bar that is sponsoring the race. Keep them away.

    Make sure their equipment is adequate for the task, does it carry all their food? Can it store a windbreaker or emergency blanket? Is it old and at risk of breaking on the course? Have they trained long enough to break in their new shoes?

Ultra-Distance Races

- Distance: 30M+/50k+
- Avg time to complete: 12 - 24hrs depends on if it is a time trial or distance race. Some Ultras are as many laps as possible in 24 hrs.

Photo: Spartan Media Team

About This Race:

A good example is the Spartan Ultra

The Spartan Ultra is 30 miles (50k) through rugged and usually mountainous terrain along with 60+ Obstacles

The Ultra has strict distance and cut off times you must meet to continue if you want to compete at the elite level, open waves have no cut off times.

There is a Pit Stop after the first loop. The pit stop is so you can eat, change clothes and address injuries or gear issues.

You will need a Hydration pack, Nutrition, night gear and a pit stop care package. A Pit Stop bin may possibly be packed with a change of clothes, food, and medical gear. You may also have a person to help you at the midway pit stop unless specifically stated otherwise.

A percentage of racers do not get out of the pit stop area due to injuries, poor food choices, GI issues or just fatigue or feeling of defeat.

Elites finish the UB in 8-10 hours or faster in some cases.

Cut off is 15 hours to complete

Common Obstacles

Expect all obstacles to make an appearance.

Sometimes due to the large distance some obstacles or penalties are lessened or changed. Such as having a penalty loop instead of burpees.

Terrain will play a large role as an obstacle over such a long distance. Repeated hill climbs will take an immense toll on the racer.

- **Terrain**

Usually, multiple loops on a mountain or ski resort.

Depending on Location (such as Iceland) the weather can be an extreme factor on the course.

- **Training tips**

Lots and lots of time on your feet hiking 3000-4000 ft mountains, Mountain running, long slow distance work

Just be strong enough and have a great strength to weight ratio. Light, strong and mobile is the way to go at this distance.

- **Training Time**

10-16 weeks

- **Coaches Notes**

With training time this long, injuries are more likely to crop up. Especially IT band syndrome, piriformis syndrome, and plantar fasciitis. Make sure your athlete(s) are paying attention to their mobility, recovery and taking care of their feet.

10

THE MENTAL SIDE
(PSYCHOLOGY OF AN OCR)

Photo/Athlete: J. Moss

I am not a sports psychologist, but I hope that my experiences as a racer and coach will be helpful to you. One of the first things I advise doing, even before the race specific tips, is to define what success in this space looks like to you. Is success just completing a race, no matter how long? Is it completing all obstacles without a penalty? Or perhaps just showing up every day to train or make it to the start line? Only you can set your goal line and measure of success.

Defining what it means to be successful, or your end goal will make the choices along the way very clear as to what you need to do versus getting distracted by the next thing or training program. Should I run more? Eat this cake? Work on strength? Distance? To answer those small choices all you need to ask is "will this get me to my goal?" Or "Is this what I need to do to be successful?" This will take a great deal of stress and mental work of your brain and nervous system. This will also lead to your driving force or purpose for doing an obstacle course race.

When something unexpected hits and will potentially derail your training or may make you think about quitting in the middle of a race, you will have a strong anchoring point to hold onto and keep moving forward. Most success is just not quitting. Not talent, resources, or ability. It's usually perseverance and grit as well as knowing where you are going and why you are doing it.

The Endurance Mindset

What you are about to do is hard. It is hard on purpose. The good thing is that you know this and once you accept this fact it will become easier. The endurance mindset is a shift in thinking. It is a change from thinking about the finish line to the process of getting to the finish line. The journey, the struggle, the challenge is what makes the finish line a beautiful thing. If you worry about when you will be done, or how far it is to the end you will suffer the whole way.

Instead enjoy the process of the race. The completion of each challenge is a success. Some of the best moments in a race come when you stop to look at the view after a challenging and grueling hike to the top. Enjoy the process and take in the experience, it can be life changing.

Going Long Distance

Let's face it, running for a long time can get boring. So how do we deal with a long run that doesn't seem exciting? This is usually the case with ½ marathon and longer distances. Luckily the Obstacle Course Races have lots of things to break up the running parts! I like to think of it as getting to play for long distances. For most athletes training for a longer race the tedium starts to set in after the 7-8 Mile training runs have been completed. Here are a few things to keep your mind on point and focused during long runs

Using Music

For any training run longer than 7 miles I suggest making a custom playlist with music that is set to a similar BPM target as my running cadence for that distance. I personally use electronic music as it's easy to find the proper BPM and it doesn't distract me from staying focused on running. Music with words makes me daydream and I tend to trip when I am not paying attention.

As you get closer to the race it is best to get used to running without music. You will not want to submerge your music device under muddy water, lose it in the mud or distract yourself during the race.

Beware falling into using music as a crutch. Things go wrong, batteries die, and devices break. Relying on an external device to keep you going is setting yourself up for failure. Practice developing the internal fortitude to keep moving without music.

Trail Running

Trail running is inherently conducive to staying present in the moment and engaged on your runs. If you are not in the moment you may run into something or trip. This is great for building the endurance mindset. Stay aware on the trail and in the race. While you are running, practice mindfulness and sustained focus. Be aware of your breathing and body.

Bodyweight Movements

To help build the endurance mindset we can make the runs more challenging. Every few miles I put in a series of pushups, sit ups, squats, Lunges, or my favorite Burpees. I like to pick 3 and do 10 reps each spread out over a run. Pick a distance and movement to do like "Every 1 mile I will do 10 pushups". You may not want to do this at first. Remember that developing a mindset is like developing a muscle and it must be exercised as well.

Carry Something Heavy

Some of the most challenging moments in a race will come while you are carrying a sandbag or heavy object. Your mindset will determine if you stay on that course and finish or put the weight down and walk away.

Get comfortable doing hard things. Wear a weight vest on hikes, carry a heavy rock or bucket uphill for a long period of time. Know that you can endure with the correct attitude, mindset and pacing.

Slow/Fast

Long runs tend to beat up the muscle groups you are using. I like to pick some spots to open the speed and stretch out the legs for a bit. Nothing too much, just enough to make the legs feel good and switch gears for a bit. Uphill/downhill sprints can be great to add into longer/slower runs. Using this method helps develop the mindset and feeling that you can do more even when tired.

Pacing with the endurance mindset

You need to go the distance. To do so your training, pacing and mindset need to be in alignment with the distance you want to go. Proper pacing for long distances can be gauged in multiple ways.

1) Race pace or target time

2) Heart rate.

3) Breathing pattern

1. It can be mentally challenging if you are chasing the wrong metric for pacing and distance. You need to match the right metric up to the right goal for your training session or race. Most new long-distance runners tend to chase the time per mile or average pace. This can sometimes be hard to hold if you choose the wrong pace to run at. The only time to go all out is during intervals.

    When doing tempo runs leave something in the tank. For long runs work on staying slow. For each of these your mind or body may urge you to do something else, especially during the slow runs. Do your best to stick to the plan.

2. Monitoring heart rate can be helpful to keep track of during training runs. You will want to stay in the aerobic zone on longer runs. If you are not tracking it you may go into a threshold run or anaerobic zone because you "Feel Good" only later to feel like you cannot finish due to feeling "gassed" or if you hit a wall due to poor fuel timing because you burned through too much energy too early. This can lead you to think you may not be a good enough runner. Sometimes a Slow run will mean Really slow and almost walking due to having to stay in the aerobic zone.

3. Monitor your breathing pattern. Breathing on long runs should be relaxed and allow you to speak and talk with a running partner. If your breathing is too labored, you will need to have the will to slow down. This is not as easy as it sounds for some runners.

    "Where does it go? ... "It Goes Up!" - Ghostbusters

When participating in an OCR with high elevation or long inclines one of the things I see break athletes is the constant up and down on a mountain. Sometimes the "Death March" (a mile straight up the mountain) can get an athlete in a negative mind space. An athlete needs to not only be in good physical condition to go long distances uphill but mentally prepared for the climbs as well. There are a few mental tricks I recommend using for long climbs up a mountain.

1. Choose consistent markers to meet

I like to choose a rock or tree about 30 - 50 ft up the trail to make it too before stopping to rest. This gives me small manageable goals to meet, gives me success and permission to take a breath. I make it a point to smile every time I stop and to set my sights on the next goal up the trail. When I am with teammates, we generally take turns choosing the markers to reach and make it a fun cooperative game as well as gives us a chance to cheer each other onward.

2. Have a positive mantra or a song

I choose something that will keep me positive and upbeat. Lately, I have been repeating the song "Everything is Awesome…" from the Lego Movie, But I have also used others like "smile", "I love the challenge", "One foot in front of the other" etc… Remind yourself that you are here for the challenge, you are alive and grateful for it. Negativity can really stop your forward momentum and make the experience harder than it needs to be. Positivity and negativity are extremely infectious on the course. Would you rather be next to someone that is complaining and negative or having a good time in the face of adversity?

Coaches Notes

If you are leading a group, they will be looking to you for cues on how to feel and react in the face of adversity. Practice Stoicism and stay encouraging. Keep the group's eye on the horizon and choose the spots to move to such as saying, "10 more steps to that tree then we can breathe".

The moment you as a leader break down the group will feel they have permissions to as well. Once the group loses the focus and forward momentum it is hard to get it back.

Obstacles and The Mind

Obstacles are designed to be challenging but also trigger a primal response or reaction. Experiencing these fears can sometimes cause difficulty for a racer.

Sometimes fear can affect us before we even sign up for a race, such as "Oh that looks too tough", "I can't do that", "I can't get dirty" or "I have never been able to run that far". After getting over the initial fear of signing up for a race here are some of the biggest fears I see while training athletes and some guidance on moving past them.

Fear of not completing an obstacle

Sometimes we can be so afraid of seeing an obstacle, whether on video or in person, that we do not even attempt it.

Fear of heights/climbing

Start on the ground and practice the obstacle in parts. Have a support or safety structure in place (like crash pads) to reduce the risk factor. Usually, it is not the obstacle we are fearful of but the possibility of what may happen if we fail the obstacle (falling).

Fear of injury

Sometimes these fears can stop you (them) from signing up for a race before you (they) even start. Fear is okay, but a plan to conquer the fear is important. Trust in a team can help support conquering one's fear. Training can be a huge help in getting over fear. The more we see and practice an obstacle in parts or in its whole the more familiar we are and the less fear we will have.

Dealing with Heights

Whether small or large, some athletes will feel butterflies when climbing obstacles. A fear of heights is natural. If you know you have a fear of heights this is where gradual training can help prepare you.

In the case of a rope climb you can get comfortable with the technique at a ground level and start training your eyes to focus on the rope and not looking down.

Focus or look at something close, like your hands or a part of the obstacle. Avoid looking at things in the distance. Focus on the process of moving forward such as one hand in front of the other or saying what you are doing to yourself (move hand, move foot, move forward)

The Pressure of Accuracy

Most misses with accuracy-based obstacles, like a spear throw, can be avoided by resting slightly before to get your heart rate down to a resting BPM before attempting. Work on a process that will give you a solid start

Observe - Make sure the obstacle is set up correctly and there are no obstructions to finishing the obstacle such as a missing knot on a rope or a tangled line on a Spartan spear

Breathe - Slow down your heart rate if needed

Align - Make sure you are set up properly from the start and you know where the target is. You are facing the correct direction

Aim - Point where you are throwing

Throw - Follow through properly and give it your best effort

This simple process may take 30 to 40 seconds but save you 2+ mins of penalty burpees or an extra lap.

Grit

What is "Grit" and why is it important?

Grit is a character trait that can be developed. It is the ability to endure harsh or challenging conditions of the mind and body while pushing through to an end goal.

The ability to keep moving forward toward a goal. In an OCR grit could be just not quitting or attempting an obstacle even though you are scared or have failed it in the past. Grit is the core of the endurance mindset. The shift from the desire to remove the immediate discomfort to the acceptance of discomfort and a commitment to the long slow drive to the finish line. I will outline a few ways to develop grit in training and an OCR.

When it Sucks, Keep Going

Delayed gratification is one of the factors that helps determine the "grit" factor of an athlete. Can you gut out one more bear crawl or burpee? Can you delay quitting and finish the race? This is an extremely important trait to have for the 10+M races or multi lap races. Doing multiple heavy sandbags or bucket-carries up a steep hill can create a strong reason for any athlete to give up. You need to have a bigger reason for completing the race than quitting.

Have a Plan for Failure?

Accept that there is a possibility of failure. It is okay and part of the experience of an OCR. When you fail an obstacle, or your initial plan fails, have a backup plan or a plan for failure. Failure is not the end or a reason to quit but a way that just didn't work. There are many ways to success, but you must explore them as not all the ways work at all times. Once you have accepted the chance of failure you can manage your expectations and still smile at the outcome.

Regroup

Sometimes a team member may quit on the intended goal. Regroup and recharge your energy. Motivate and focus on something attainable. Perhaps you feel fatigued or unmotivated at some point in the race. It's okay to gather your strength by resting and reciting your mantras or just commiserating in a positive way with your teammates.

Reassess

Give yourself a new angle of attack by thinking differently or creatively. Perhaps you failed an obstacle. What was the weak link? If it is an open heat (noncompetitive) after you have completed your penalty go back and attempt the obstacle again. Try it a different way or get help. In the case of a wall, it may take a team to scale it.

Give yourself a smaller/closer goal

In a long uphill march or a long heavy carry, the distance just mentally feels too hard and too far to travel. Instead of giving up and abandoning the challenge, focus on choosing a shorter distance to travel. Stop and rest, choose a new target distance and move again.

Have a Strong or Personal Mantra

Having a Mantra or positive saying that reinforces why you are there is important. Practice it in training, link it to a very strong memory, person, or feeling. Attach it to your "WHY", why you are there, why you started and why you will finish. A Mantra should help you stay positive, focused and aware/present as well as give you strength.

One I use is repeating "Everything is Awesome" from the LEGO® Movie. It's a positive memory with my children, it's fun to think about, it's a bit ironic considering the situation usually, and it's short and repeatable (just like in the movie).

Your mantra does not have to be as lighthearted, but it does have to help you, be short and repeatable and put you in a positive frame of mind.

I have found that there can be a lot of negativities on the longer races from people that are not prepared. Your mantra will help shield you from other people's negativity and save you from getting dragged down into a bad head space.

Smile, Your Outlook Depends on it

Smiling will help you and those around you. Smiling will keep your spirits up and thoughts positive. Smiling helps us shine a light on the positive things of the challenge. Perhaps you just finished a long heavy climb or are in the middle of a long heavy carry. Smile and look around. Enjoy the view and take in the shared experience so many others are going through with you. When others see you smiling, they will forget about their own discomfort for a bit and join in. Perhaps it's a good chance to share some food, the view or just good company before heading to the next challenge.

Support Others

Help and gratitude will change how you feel. If you are resting or if others on your team are struggling, help them out by offering words of encouragement. It's always good to know that someone sees and recognizes the struggle we are all going through. It lets us know we are in it together. By helping others, we help ourselves.

11

OBSTACLE SPECIFIC TRAINING

Photo: A. Wisch

With the rise of the TV show Ninja Warrior and Televised Obstacle Course races more and more people want to train on obstacles and in obstacle centric gyms. Some obstacles are hard to conquer on a course without training or instruction. Some can seem like a puzzle to solve.

You can build most obstacles yourself if you want to get some experience training on them.

There are now indoor trampoline parks, Gymnastics studios, Ninja Warrior style gyms and OCR specific gyms all with obstacles to train on. Finding one in your area can give you experience needed on the course. Most people seek out a gym to get hands-on instruction on rope climbing, wall climbing, spear throwing etc. These gyms are also great to find a like-minded training environment to train for an upcoming race.

Remember that the obstacles themselves are there to only test your strength, grip and endurance. Most people just lack the basic strength to complete obstacles, after learning the techniques you should be able to complete most obstacles if you are strong enough. Do not trade Obstacle training for basic strength and conditioning. Obstacles are just puzzles to solve using your strength, grip, agility, coordination and endurance. Too much time practicing obstacles will lead to overuse injuries.

Developing Obstacle Immunity

The best way to conquer any obstacle is to build a wide base of strength, flexibility and endurance. Most of these courses swap out obstacles from year to year and the innovative races try to put new twists on the obstacles. Such as adding moving parts (spinning monkey bars), or changing the conditions of the obstacle (thinner ropes).

Having a flexible and strong body as well as mindset will be the best way to give you obstacle immunity. Stay focused on the course and do not take an obstacle for granted. No matter the type of obstacle they throw at you, you will need to be confident in your body to tackle it. It would be unfortunate to over train a specific obstacle to only get to a race and it is not there or have a different variation. What do you do then? If you have built a broad skill set, worked on flexibility, mobility, and stability you will be able to adapt to any obstacle on the course.

First, you need to be strong but not bulky. A good strength to weight ratio is important. You will need to be able to pick up heavy objects and carry them as well as pull your own body weight over a wall or up a rope and still be able to run long distances. You will need to be able to support your weight hanging with one arm.

For strength work, focus on Single leg and arm exercises such as split squats (sometimes called Bulgarian or rear elevated leg split squats) over the traditional back squat, deadlift or presses. A few examples would be single leg deadlifts, single arm kettlebell or dumbbell presses, swings and snatches. This does not mean that I dislike the traditional lifts, in fact I love them for off season strength training or even in HIIT style workouts or Metabolic Conditioning (MetCon) workouts. You can keep in the traditional back squat, deadlift, and presses but start to add in single limb movements into your main strength work or as accessory movements.

Hanging obstacles require a great deal of strength through a huge range of motion (ROM). Most people do not have the prerequisite shoulder ROM before trying to hang their entire body weight on one arm. We first need to develop a proper range of motion. Here are some self-tests you can do:

- Can you get your bicep to your ear without having to compensate?
- Does your rib cage flare up or do you have to arch your back when you reach overhead?
- Can you hang from both arms and keep your shoulders active (away from your ears)?
- Does your head sink down into your shoulders?
- Work towards being able to maintain a strong shoulder position while hanging as well as being able to engage your core.

Gymnasts call this the "hollow body" position. Work on hanging from a pull up bar with a tight body for time. Work towards one minute hang time on the bar. In the beginning start with :10s - :20s holds and increase up to a total of 1 minute over time. After you feel strong in the hang position, you can start to move through a hanging range of motion (ROM). Gymnasts call this the beat swing.

The Beat Swing engages our lats, shoulders and core in a dynamic motion moving forward and backwards in the hang position. Next, can we release one arm under control while hanging. Start with first trying to release one hand from the bar. It doesn't have to move far from the bar. If you are confident that you can release and touch your chest or hip and place it back on the bar and repeat on the other side. This will require excellent grip strength and body control. This is useful for hanging obstacles that do not have anything for you to secure your feet to and push off. You will be able to use your body movement to swing into a pull up or get your leg up onto the obstacle.

The Mountain/Terrain

This is usually the most limiting factor for most people and what tends to truly separate the elite from the crowd. Uphill training, elevation training, proper gear and experience can play a big part in a race with elevation.

Why does it take an elite racer 4 hours to run a Spartan Beast on Mt Killington in Vermont but racers in the open waves 8 hours? These elite athletes have dialed in their level of training for incline runs, heavy hikes, and nutrition. They have simply spent more time training for inclines and total elevation.

Races on ski mountains are the easiest to account for as each mountain's elevation is published on their websites. Racers routinely publish their distance and elevation maps on previous courses. Check the venue for your race and the elevation gain of the mountains. If the elevation gain is 1000' then you need to be conditioned to move uphill for 1000'. I can guarantee that if you are not training enough elevation to cover the ascents of a race, cramping will start to happen at the limit of your training.

Training for the Elevation/Mountains

Leg conditioning tools/methods:

- **Hills**

    Work on walking then running uphill. Even if the hill is not as high in elevation as the race you can do multiple ascents in a setting. If you need to cover 1000' of elevation but your hill only covers 200', work up 5 sets of ascents without stopping. 5x200' = 1000'. I also like to add in a bit more ascent training than the race may call for to make sure there is more in the tank.

- **Sleds**

    Pushing and pulling sleds are excellent leg training methods. You can go fast or slow, light or heavy. A good target to work towards is being able to push your body weight added to a sled for 100m without stopping.

- **Lunges**

    Lunges are often not done enough in training. Practice static holds for time, forward lunges, reverse lunges, walking lunges, lunges with weight, up and down small hills. Lunges can also make a great finisher for any workout. Do 50 - 100 lunges after a workout session.

    Find a soccer or football field and lunge across. Take breaks if needed but time yourself and see how long it takes you to get across the field. Work on getting across without stopping then work on going back. Every time you complete a full field without stopping to add an additional lap.

- **Stadium Stairs**

  High school fields or College Stadiums are a great alternative to hills, especially if you are training for a stadium race like Fenway or Citi Field. A City or high school football or track field will have bleachers or stairs that you can run up and down. A college stadium (such as Harvard stadium) is a big oval, and each section has a flight of stairs.

  Work towards completing each stair section around the whole stadium. Start by walking the stadium stairs first and time yourself. After you can complete the entire stadium walking try to run 10 - 20% of the stairs or sections and walk the rest. Add 5-10% every week. Do stadium stairs only 1-2x a week until you can run the entire stadium.

  Bring a friend and be prepared to walk funny for a few days.

- **Treadmills**

  Trails and roads are better for training but if a treadmill is your only option follow a few guidelines.

  Most treadmills are not built for uphill running. There are a few models that are made for extreme incline training. It is best to fast walk/hike on an inclined treadmill then running.

  Try to run softly, do not stomp on the treadmill. If simulating a hill some treadmills have a hill setting or hill interval setting. Use that but try walking/hiking first. See how far you can go for 45 mins. Add in a sandbag, bucket, or light ruck/backpack carry to add some challenge to a treadmill session.

- **Jacob's Ladder**

  Jacob's Ladder is a great OCR conditioning machine. It is essentially an infinite ladder that is at a 40-degree lean. It is like climbing a ladder or crawling up a hill for as long as you want. Start off slowly using this as coordination is required. Start with slow climbs for a minute and rest a minute. This machine will simulate the bear crawls and A-Frame climbs in the races.

- **Obstacle Grip Strength**

Every race requires a great deal of not only grip strength but grip endurance and stamina. Some race designers love to stack multiple grips killing obstacles close together to burn out your hands and forearms. This makes each successive one harder to complete if you are attempting to go fast. Grip strength in most cases is quick to return. Especially if you are waiting between obstacles and taking your time.

Here are some movements that help build great OCR grip strength. I suggest that you vary up your tools every 2-3 weeks and be sure to stop if you develop any issues with the elbows or wrists.

Maximal lifts (ex: 1 rep max) are not necessary for OCR. Heavy lifts can be helpful in the off seasons to help build top end strength but are not as useful for in season obstacle course races. Strength endurance (10-20 reps per set or 1-2 mins of exertion) is more beneficial for the OCR racer. We need to be strong while moving for a long time. This means that weights will be between 50-70% of max efforts.

If you have a long off season between race seasons then that is a great time to work up to heavy weights such as sets of 5, 3 or 1 reps or between 70-90% max efforts. Start to lower the heavy weight 6-8 weeks out before your first race and start to increase the reps (ex. 8, 10, 20 reps).

Varying the type of grip is very useful. Change the diameter and orientation of the grip. You can do this by changing up the implement used or adding something to the handle to make it thicker. A great grip exercise is to use towels to lift objects or to hang onto from a pullup bar.

Grip Strength Movements

Deadlifts

The deadlift is simply "picking heavy stuff up". Using a Barbell, dumbbell or kettlebell for this movement will all help build great grip strength. To build grip strength using this movement use different tools. Use thick handled kettlebells, different size dumbbells, a barbell or a hex bar. Don't get used to one type of thickness or weight. There are companies that sell foam grips that go over the barbell or DB/KB grips

Kettlebell Swings

A grip building exercise for sure! Your grip will get taxed long before your legs when done right. Kettlebell swings are great for building grip endurance, you can get in a lot of volume with them. The basic is the two-handed swing which you can get up to a heavy amount of weight swinging but for grip work you will want to keep to a moderate weight and work on the length of time swinging the bell.

To get an even greater focus on the grip use the one-handed swing. You can swing on the same side or alternate hands midair. The one-handed swing will allow you to maximize each hand to its fullest to build grip strength.

An advanced 2 handed variation to build grip strength with the kettlebell is the towel swing. Place a 2-foot towel through the handle and grip tightly the ends of the towel like handles. The kettlebell will be farther away from you so the arc will be different. Start the swing slow and work your way up to a full swing as you get used to the greater arc of the swing. Grip the towel tightly so it does not slip out of your hands at the top of the swing.

Plate Pinch Carries

The plate pinch carry is a great finger strength exercise. Pick up a thick, smooth plate with your thumbs and fingertips. You can stand and hold for time or walk while holding the plates. Start with an easy plate and progress to a heavier plate over time.

Farmers Walks

The Farmer Walk can be done with anything that has a handle you can grip and carry. The most used implements are dumbbells and kettle-bells. Simply pick them up, set your posture and walk as far as you can go before putting them down.

Hangs

Working on hanging strength is a must in obstacle course racing. You will need to be able to support your whole body hanging from both hands as well as one hand. You may not be able to hang very long at first so do short, timed intervals to build hand and shoulder strength. As your grip strength improves so should your hanging time.

Rock Climbing

Rock climbing is a great way to have fun and build some good climbing and grip strength. You do not need to top rope as bouldering is fine for this. In bouldering there is an exercise called a 4x4. To do a 4x4 choose 4 bouldering routes that are relatively easy, attempt to complete each route 4 times without stopping.

Ground Obstacles

These are obstacles that require crawling and/or getting down on the ground. Many will require you to get dirty and play in the mud, others will require you to crawl through an obstacle.

Obstacle	Barbed Wire Crawls
Description	Low crawl obstacle. Barbed wire or rope is suspended over pprox.. 100-200m of the course. You will need to crawl under the obstacle to the end.
Training	I include various methods of crawling into all my warmups. Variation is key. Work on Bear crawls, army crawls, shrimp crawls, Inch worms, rolling (forward, backward, log roll). Put a few of them in each warmup and rotate them each week. In your workouts include low crawls under objects or through objects such as run-crawl-climb etc.
Race Day	Crawling under barbed wire or ropes is an obstacle that for some has become the most difficult and taxing of all the obstacles. It is hard to move fast, and your gear/clothing/body can get caught on the barbs. Most races intend for you to keep all your gear with you as you go under the wire. If possible/ allowed in your race put your hydration packs at the end of the wire and go back to the start. Make sure that your hydration pack mouthpiece is secured. I watched my teammate's mouthpiece get caught on a barb and empty all his water out. **Rolling:** Rolling under barbed wire works well until you get dizzy or hit a rock or hole. Use it when you can but be aware of hitting others and switch sides. Do not rely solely on this method as race designers have started to build in natural obstacles to challenge this method. Such as up/down hill, adding in holes and dirt mounds. Also, there is a chance you could make yourself too dizzy or ill from lots of rolling. If this is your only method, then when you switch to a different crawling pattern/style you will cramp or get injured. **Bear Crawl:** If the barbed wire or ropes are high enough, I recommend using the bear crawl method. They are usually high enough near the support poles for an average height athlete to use this method (under 6' tall). You can move quickly on your hands and feet/knees. If you have a pack on you will be at risk of catching it on the barbs. I have also seen long hair that was unsecured get caught as well.
Coach Notes	Do not go too fast, especially on the rolling. Fast rolling requires some acclimation to the movement, so your balance center doesn't freak out and cause vertigo and motion sickness. If you have not practiced this in training to determine your actual threshold on how fast and how far you can do it, I would avoid speed rolling. You will only end up worse for wear by the end of the obstacle.

Obstacle	Pipe crawls
Description	These are large plastic drainage pipes used in construction. They have an opening diameter of roughly 24 – 30". This will require most people to crawl on their hands and knees to get through. If the pipe is angled or vertical It will be challenging to apply enough force into the walls to crawl up and through the pipe, especially if it is wet or muddy.
Training	Start by setting up pvc pipes or ropes horizontal at 24" off the ground. Crawl under for 6-10' distances. Add these into work-outs between movements. For lateral pressing you can practice door frame holds. Press your arms into a doorway and then step your feet one by one into the door frame suspending yourself off the floor. If the doorway or hallway is narrow enough you can attempt to shimmy up the sides.
Race Day	During a race, take your time getting through the pipes. If you rush and slip or get injured, you will lose more time than if you went through at a moderate but secure pace.
Coach Notes	Use a controlled speed, trying to go through the pipes fast can lead to an injury. The most common mistake is not making sure you have good traction. Feet and hands slip inside the pipes which lead to your knees and elbows taking some damage or you are sliding backwards if they are angled. I also see racers not get low enough going in and hit their back on the edges as well as on the way out they stand up too soon and hit their back again.

Water Obstacles

Water obstacles can severely break a racer if not ready for them. The biggest problem is the extreme temperature difference between the air and water. This can cause bad cramping in the legs. Most beginner level races tend to avoid having them as obstacles for this reason. Most races will have the small ankle or waist high mud puddles they make you go through to get dirty and mildly uncomfortable. The bigger races may require life vests and swimming.

Obstacle	Dunk Wall
Description	A 5' wall submerged 2' into a large reservoir of muddy water. The athletes must submerge themselves and go under the wall to the other side.
Training	If you have access to a pool, you can have a friend hold their hand a few feet under the water and you can practice submerging and transitioning under an obstacle in a safe environment.
Race Day	Reach under and find the end of the wall with your hand. Hold onto it and use it to guide you to the other side. The water is muddy, and you will not be able to see. Using your hands has the added benefit in speeding up this transition so you are not under water very long. Using your hands will tell you where you are under the water and if you have gone under the wall. I have seen racers dive under without grabbing the end and either come up too soon, thereby having to try again, or bump their head into or on the wall. If you are wearing a hydration pack, take it off and throw it to the side of the water on the land. Most new racers get their pack caught on the wall because they are rushing to get under it and do not go deep enough. Most people have a psychological fear of dunking underwater. If you are uncomfortable with going under the water, you can avoid this one. Some people find it easier to do this with a friend for the first time to get under safely.
Coach Notes	Know where the wall is. I have seen racers take a deep breath, close their eyes, and go under only to come back up on the same side because they didn't know where they were going. Make sure you put a hand on or under the wall before you go under.

Obstacle	Ice Dunk
Description	This is like the wall dunk but is ice water, as in water with ice cubes poured into it. To say it's cold is putting it mildly. This is one that can usually be skipped if you had a condition that would lead to hypothermia or the weather conditions would keep you from warming up. This will also make most people cramp up after they come out. I do not suggest going right into a run after this obstacle. This is as much of a mental obstacle as a physical one. As you may have to mentally force your body to start moving after coming out.
Training	Train for this on a warm or hot weather day. Set up a large bin outside and add lots of ice, so the top of the water is covered by ice. Do some short sprints and body weight exercises then submerge yourself in an ice bath. Get out and start moving again. Do this 3-5 times.

Race Day	Be mentally ready for the cold plunge, stay calm and do not let your nerves get out of control.
Coach Notes	Do not start running too soon after getting out. Extreme cold will cause cramping. Take some time to warm up your body by rubbing your hands all over. Try to get your core temperature up before getting back into a run. This may mean walking or jogging for a short bit. Do not stand still, keep moving.

Obstacle	Water Crossing – Short Distance, Shallow
Description	Waist high or lowers water hazards or streams that you can wade through. The make-up of the water can vary from clear to muddy.
Training	Training can be done in a pool or any body of water between knee and mid chest height. Between sets of exercises walk for 1-3 minutes forcefully through the water.
Race Day	Try to keep your pack out of the water if possible. Especially if you have food there. Good drainage in your shoes is important here.
Coach Notes	Water hazards of this type are there to slow you down. Depending on the terrain under the water there can be a potential injury waiting to happen. Take your time, everyone is going to go slow here. You can only move quickly through water when the water line is at a joint level (ankle, knee, waist). If it is not, you will spend lots of energy just moving through the water. Getting out of the water is where I see most injuries and cramping occur. Do not rush to get out. Plan your exit route out of the water to avoid running into another racer or slipping on rocks and roots.

Obstacle	Water Crossing – Long Distance, Deep
Description	The longer water hazards usually require a life vest and swimming. In some races this is only skippable with a penalty. These can show up in the longer races and usually towards the middle of the race.
Training	Training for this obstacle I suggest adding some short swims to your training. Like Triathlon "brick" training. Run-swim-run. Adding this in is only needed if your race will include it such as a 24 hr. endurance series or long form race. Mountain races will have cold water. You can train for this by going in and out of ice baths or cold showers between movements. Caution: have supervision or someone trained in spotting hypothermia even in warm weather.

Race Day	Stay relaxed, swimming can lead to some major cramping and fatigue. If you are not a good swimmer, I suggest adding in a few training swims throughout the year to improve your comfort level. Let the life vest do its work so you can recover some energy. Some races will have an obstacle as part of the water hazard. Sometimes a hanging obstacle under a bridge or a floatation traverse (walking over boats or foam boards in the water). Some extreme and longer races (12 to 24 hrs.) will require a wetsuit, do your research and get the right wetsuit for you and that specific race and that you train multiple times in the suit. Some racers have reported overheating due to the wrong suit.
Coach Notes	Do not rush during the swim portion, no need to run into the water or dive in. Walk/wade into the water gradually as it will most likely be a shock to your system. Especially if the water is colder than the air temperature. Do not try to sprint swimming, you may need to have energy to complete an obstacle in the water or to warm back up to continue running.

Hanging Obstacles

Hanging Obstacles are ones that require the athlete to hang from their hands and support their entire body weight while moving forward. They may require the athlete to move through various planes as well as through various gripping implements such as bars, balls, ropes, rings, etc.

Hanging obstacles seem to be the most difficult for athletes on race day. This is usually because of a few factors. Strength to weight ratio, shoulder ROM, Core engagement or lack of, Grip strength, and strategy. Be careful dismounting from hanging obstacles.

Obstacle	Monkey Bars
Description	Horizontal bars about 7-8' in the air spaced approximately 3' from each other for a 15-20' length. Sometimes they are spaced at different heights.
Training	The first test I run my athletes through in the gym is if they can hang on a bar and keep their shoulders away from their ears. Then we test how long they can hang from the bar. Athletes should work up to a minimum of a 1-minute dead hang on the bar with good form. Next, we work on a hanging hollow body hold. Can the athlete hang with their core and lats engaged? If your core, lats and legs are not engaged during the monkey bars you will be carrying dead weight with just your arms and shoulders. Loose core and legs will drag you off the bar even if you have a strong grip. In the gym we practice what gymnasts call a "hollow" body position. Meaning my core is tight, and shoulders, lats and legs are engaged. This should look like if I was laying on the ground and slightly lifted my arms and feet off the ground and "crunched" my abs. Try it on the ground first and then get on the bar. If you have Monkey bars to train on work on going across minimizing your leg swing and keeping the shoulders and core engaged. Then work on long arm swings, brachiating like an ape swing. And then work on sideways traversing (palms facing each other) No Monkey bars: If you do not have monkey bars or a kids park nearby you will need a tree branch or pull up bar to practice hanging on. The traverses are harder to practice with just one bar. Here are some exercises to do on a single bar. Hand releases and taps: Start in a dead hang, lift one hand off the bar and then back, repeat with the other side. This should have a 1:1 rhythm like a march. Try to minimize swaying by keeping a tight core. Legs can be straight or bent. Once you can do this for :30s work on body taps. Start with shoulder taps. Release from the bar and touch your shoulder quickly, alternating hands. Next would-be chest taps and then hip taps. Try to stay quick and minimize hanging and swinging. Grip switch: work on rotating your grip. Start palms forward then turn one hand towards you and grab the bar, then the next hand. Palms should be facing you now. Turn your hands back to face forward. Keep alternating forward and backward grips for :30s

Race Day	In a race the monkey bars can vary greatly. From thick to thin bars. Lateral to angled as well as uneven distribution of distances between the bars. I like to go to the side, close to the bar supports. There is less chance of bounce in the bar, and you are guaranteed to not have someone on one side of you. I do see some racers fall off the bars because a racer next to them is flailing and kicks them off. It's unfortunate but it does happen so give yourself some room. Depending on the type of monkey bars I will change how I grab the bar. For thin bars I go palms forward with a slight arm bend moving one hand after the other. For thicker bars that I may have trouble getting a grip on I prefer to go sideways with my palms facing each other. I will swing, reach and grab with my dominant side first and then bring my other hand to the bar. This also works well for uneven bars as I can get some momentum and pull myself up to the next bar if it is above.
Coach Notes	Most beginner athletes do not have enough upper body strength and endurance in the arms, shoulders, and upper back. As well as not having a strong enough core or latissimus dorsi strength to sustain a long hold. I advise working on these weekly.

Obstacle	Ring Swing
Description	The ring swing is a series of 8-10 gymnastics rings set up in a horizontal line about 8 ft off the ground. The athlete must swing from one ring to the next without touching the ground. When the athlete reaches the other side (sometimes ringing a bell) they have completed the obstacle.
Training	In training you should be able to hang from a gymnastics ring with one arm comfortably for about 10s each arm. Work on transitioning between 2 rings at first. There are 2 methods of going through this obstacle 1) the long brachiating traverse, this is a long arm reach such as chimpanzees use when swinging. It has a long pendulum arc and arm reach. This method may allow you to skip every other ring if done properly. 2) Bent arm, the bent arm is a short and fast reach. This requires great core and arm control as well as a good fast transition to each ring. Sometimes rings are spaced far enough away that you will need to have a small swing by pulling on the rings to create a back swing before moving to the next ring.

Race Day	If you are unsure about the rings during the race, go to the side and watch people go through. Make sure that your arm reach can make it to the next ring. Some rings could be higher or lower than others. Choose the right lane for you and your arms.
Coach Notes	If keeping the arms long and swinging from hand to hand, it's best to first go back a bit to get some momentum in your swing. You need to have a good grip on the ring and be able to hold your bodyweight. It is also important to relax on the swing and time the grab properly. When swinging with long arms you may be able to skip a ring in the middle. If you mistime the grab or miss you may lose your momentum. Hold onto both rings and pull back and forward to give yourself a bigger swing with more momentum. With bent arms you are going from ring to ring very fast. You cannot stop. The mistake seen is lack of strength and coordination to move quickly through the rings. If you are unsure of your grip you can try to put your arms through the rings and use the bend in your elbow to hold on.

Obstacle	Multi Rig
Description	A multi rig combines multiple hanging obstacles into one obstacle approx. 20-30 foot long. It can do multiple types of hanging things to grab, swing, or climb across such as monkey bars into a rope traverse into rings and then hanging baseball/softballs. This requires multiple different grip strengths and a plan on a smart transition from one to the next.
Training	At the gym work on negative pull ups and chin ups as well as grip intensive towel chin ups/pull ups. Work on moving laterally across a pull up bar if you have access to a long one. Practice sideways traverses, forward hand over hand as well as changing grip direction while dead hanging on a bar. If you have access to different grips such as rings or hanging baseballs practice dead hangs and pull ups/chin ups on them.

| Mistakes | One of the biggest mistakes I see is athletes not having a good pattern from the start. You want to make sure that you are reaching and transitioning from one hanging obstacle to the next as efficiently as possible. If you know that a hanging obstacle, like Baseballs, is a weak area you can plan a way to minimize your time at that grip or how to bypass it.

Arm and grip strength are a constant issue at this obstacle. You need a good enough grip to hold your body weight up, arms close to 90 degrees and the stamina to move quickly through the obstacles. If you hang too long or take large time-consuming swings your grip will give out faster. |
|---|---|
| Race Day | Stop and visually see your hand pattern on the rig. What hand will you use to reach for the transitions? I also see people rush this sometimes and run into the person in front of them or get kicked off by the person next to them. So, make sure when you start you will be clear in the front and sides. |
| Coach Notes | One of the biggest mistakes I see athletes make is not having a good pattern from the start. You want to make sure that you are reaching and transitioning from one hanging obstacle to the next as efficiently as possible. If you know that a hanging obstacle, like Baseballs, is a weak area for you then you can plan a way to minimize your time at that grip or how to bypass it.

Arm and grip strength are a constant issue at this obstacle. You need a good enough grip to hold your body weight up, arms close to 90 degrees and the stamina to move quickly through the obstacles. If you hang too long or take large time-consuming swings your grip will give out faster. |

Obstacle	Twister
Description	A twisting set of handles on a rotating bar length wise. Each handle is off set from the next at about 20 degrees. So, when you grab the handle, the next handle is slightly above and angled down. Every time you grab a handle the whole set rotates.
Training	If you only have a pull up bar you can grab the bar with a hand facing hand grip (you will be looking down the length of the bar) and work on alternating your grip while keeping a 90-degree bend in your arms. This will also require a tight core, so you are not carrying "dead" weight. Play around with different styles. Going down the length of the bar facing forward, backward or laterally. See which style feels best for you. I personally find it easier and faster to go backwards. My arms are able to stay in a "V" or 90-degree position, I can keep my core engaged, and the rungs are always in the right position.
Race Day	Look for a lane that was completed successfully. This usually means that the rungs will all be in the right place for the next person to go. You do not want to get to the second set of rungs to find out they are all out of order and you are out of strength and coordination to fix it. Wait for the lane to be clear and tell the person behind you to not start until you are absolutely finished. You do not want someone jumping the gun and getting on the same twisting rungs as you.
Coach Notes	Have a plan on your hand placement or a proper strategy for your style of hand placement. Lack of upper body strength and speed will limit you. If you take too long and get tired you will fall off.

Obstacle	Ape hanger
Description	A metal ladder strung horizontally across water. Like monkey bars but connected by flexible steel wire. This is usually preceded by a rope climb to get to the ladder rungs.
Training	The ladder rungs are a thinner metal bar than the monkey bars. The rungs also will sway as you let go with one hand. In your training work on a strong one-handed hang from a bar. I like to practice the hip touch. Start with two hands on the bar. Remove one hand and touch your hip. Go back to a two-hand hold on the bar and then do the other hand/hip. Work up to 10 hip touches at first then up to 20. If reaching for the hip is too hard then shorten up the distance to touching your shoulder or chest.
Mistakes	Not enough upper strength to hang by one hand. Not enough speed or stamina to make it across. Not enough grip strength
Race Day	The metal can get quite slippery with the mud on the course. Technique can play a role in this. If you have quick hands I suggest grabbing as close to the ropes on the rung as possible. This will give you lateral stability. The speed matters so you do not over rotate the ladder to one side. Move your hands 1-2 to the same rung quickly. If you have long arm swings or go hand facing, I suggest grabbing for the middle to keep it stable.
Coach Notes	This is a wobbly monkey bar obstacle. You will need upper strength to hang by one hand. Transition quickly so you can get both hands on a rung to balance the bars and reduce sway.

Climbing Obstacles

These obstacles will require you to ascend and descend a vertical or angled surface. Some may be as short as 4' and others as high as 12' and require a team. All climbing obstacles are challenging and require good upper body strength and agility. These are the obstacles to be careful of. Falling from one of these or not being aware of your surroundings can lead to injury.

Obstacle	Climbing Walls
Description	A wall 4', 6' or 8' high that you must climb over and down the other side
Training	There are a few things we need to make sure we go over for a successful wall climb. There are different techniques for conquering a wall individually and as a team.

WALL CLIMBING TECHNIQUE BASICS

Strength
You need to be able to pull your body up the wall with your arms

Foot position
Getting a good secure foot position can make or break the climb. You need to be able to put your foot pressure into the wall. Too much downward pressure and your foot will slide down the wall, especially if it is wet and muddy.

Walking up the wall drill
Be able to hold onto the top of the wall and walk your feet up the wall until you are in a sitting or crouching position. This helps teach and reinforce how to apply foot pressure into the wall and not down.

Leg swing
Once you can hold onto the wall and can securely plant a foot on the wall you can attempt a leg swing to get your heel/foot onto the top of the wall

Single leg plant/Vault
Start by placing your foot on a large secure wall, preferably concrete. Practice pushing off the wall. Then pushing and extending upwards. Once you are comfortable with that start walking towards the wall, planting and touching up high on the wall. After that work on running at the wall, planting and jumping up the wall. Do not push away from the wall but up it. Then bring this to a climbing wall, work on running, planting and grabbing the top of the wall.

Muscle up
Once you can run, plant, and jump up the wall you can work on getting your body over the wall. With enough speed and momentum, you can grab the top with both hands simultaneously and pull your upper body over the wall similar to a Muscle Up.

Training	**Team techniques** The right way vs wrong way to get a teammate over a wall. The safest way over the wall is a team of 2-3 people. One person in the "chair position", one person on the wall, and another on the ground spotting the climber. I advise against using the "five fingers" technique or pushing a person over the wall from behind. Both methods can lead to injury for both people due to instability and to many variables that they are dependent on for success. **The chair method** This is my most advised method for teams. It does take some practice for the "chair" and the climber. This is mainly due to the climber being worried about injuring the person that they are climbing on. To start, the person that is the "chair" needs to sit with their backs against the wall. Feet about hip width, or in a comfortable position. Legs and torso will be at a 90-degree angle. The person can grab under the wall if it is within reach. The climber can start outside or inside the legs of the support person. **Inside the legs:** Place a hand on each of the support persons shoulders. Place a foot in the crook of the hip where the leg and hip meet. Put pressure into your leg on the support person and push with your hands, reach for the top of the while stepping up onto the support person (be careful not to knee them in the face here), if you can step up onto their shoulder, grab the top of the wall and climb up and over the wall **Outside the legs:** How you step up will be determined by your dominant side. You will want to step in the crook of the hip with your non-dominant side, reach for the opposite shoulder and stand up/step onto the closest shoulder. And reach for the top of the wall. Stay close to the wall. To be safe climbing a wall that is covered in mud and water you need to start in a safe clean environment and learn good technique. Climbing a wall is a whole-body task that requires upper body pulling, lower body pushing, and coordination.

Training	Start with a small wall, if possible, learn how to vault over the 4' wall. Practice laying on top of the wall. Figure out if you are right or left side dominant. Which way are you comfortable facing when on top of the wall? When you get to the larger wall do you reach up with your left or right? This might look like a layup shot in basketball. Which hand reaches for the basket? That is your dominant hand that you will use to grab the wall. Which foot do you push off? That will be the foot you place on the wall first.
	Practice hanging on the wall and pulling. Can you pull your body up? A little or a lot? If there is little to no movement, you will need to focus on proper technique and foot placement. If you can do a full pull up on the wall you may be able to use a more advanced technique called the muscle up.
	Work first on trying to "walk" up the wall and "hooking" your heel or leg over the top and using your arms and legs to pull you on top of the wall. If your feet slide down when you attempt this your hips might be either too close to the wall or too far above your feet. Make sure when you walk up the wall that you can "push" your feet into the wall. Sometimes athletes pull too early with their arms and change their center of gravity from going "into" the wall to going towards the ground. This is when the feet slip down the wall making the heel or leg hook difficult. When going over the top of the wall be careful not to kick anyone with your feet or legs. Sit or rest on the top by laying down on your chest. Survey the other side of the wall. Every injury I have seen at the wall has been dismounting too quickly or landing on uneven terrain. I like to "brake" on my way down the other side. This is down by swinging just your legs over while resting your hip or waist on top of the wall. Plant your hands and put your feet into the wall. When you push off/lower yourself down the wall push your heels into the wall and sit down while still holding onto the wall. Once your arms are extended, lower your feet and land softly.

Race Day	Always make sure that the path is clear, do not run/rush past someone to make it over the wall faster unless you are in a competitive heat. Even then it's not a good move. Always check the landing area to make sure it's clear of debris. Sometimes water hides rocks. Landing wrong will cost you the whole race.
	When teammates are trying to help you over the wall, I advocate the "chair" method instead of the "five finger" method. The chair method is stable and much safer. This technique is when a teammate sits with their backs against the wall and the athlete "steps" up then to climb over the wall.
Coach Notes	Here are a few things to watch out for.
	Make sure you slow down before a wall and check out the area for mud or water holes or rocks. Watch out for slippery surfaces before and after the wall.
	Most of the injuries that I have witnessed in person have happened coming off the wall. Don't jump down from the top. Climb down and look before you land.
	Watch out for people at the top, pay attention so you do not kick anyone or get kicked. I mostly have been kicked in the head by racers trying to get over the wall fast without any regard for other racers.
	Don't land on anyone (have patience) and watch out for rocks or uneven surfaces at the base of the wall. The worst injury I witnessed was when a racer hopped off the top of the wall and his foot landed on a small rock sticking out of the ground. It was a funny enough angle to create enough force and torsion to break their tibia bone through the skin.
	Oftentimes at races it looks like it is the first time many of the people have tried to climb a wall. Many lack the upper body pulling strength needed to make it over a wall easily. I also notice that most do not have a plan or the proper technique to climb down the wall safely or in a way that will reduce injury.
	Lastly a mistake I unfortunately see is overconfidence or rushing to get through the obstacle. This can be dangerous for other racers if they are not aware you want to fly through the obstacle at top speed. If you want to go fast, please register for the competitive heats.

Obstacle	Climbing Walls – Inverted
Description	A climbing wall that has the top angled towards the athlete pprox.. 30-45 degrees with 2x4's horizontally for stepping
Training	This is a difficult obstacle to replicate outside of the race unless you want to build your own. The closest thing would be to find a rock-climbing gym that has a bouldering wall. This will allow you to practice the stability you need to coordinate the timing of the upper and lower movements while hanging at an angle off the wall. Work on core movements in the gym like V-ups, Toes to bar, L-sit pull ups
Race Day	Be patient, try to pick the wall with the least amount of dirt/mud on it or one that is dry. To get over the lip you will need a little momentum by pulling with your arms and pushing with your legs. Climb up and grab the top lip, get your feet on the 2x4 cross support, do a little squat with straight arms to load your legs for jumping, jump and pull your body towards the top of the wall, swing and reach with your foot/leg, hook it to the top of the wall and stay close to the lip by pulling your chest to it and roll-on top.
Coach Notes	The inverted wall is tough, mentally and physically. Just trying to figure out how to climb it can be a challenge. Try it and see if you can solve the puzzle. Experience goes a long way so do not be discouraged if you don't get it the first time.

Obstacle	Rope Climb
Description	A 15'- 20' rope suspended from a truss. You must climb up the rope to ring a bell at the top
Training	The rope climb has a secret. It's mainly done with the legs and a secure anchor (foot clamp) and less climbing with the arms. Most people have trouble with the rope climb due to believing that they lack the upper body strength to accomplish it. But usually what I see is that they lack a proper anchor and leg technique going up the rope. Athletes try to pull their entire body weight up the rope. If you cannot do at least 10 strict pull ups without stopping your chances of getting up that rope with mainly your arms will be slim. However, you have strong legs that push your body weight up all day. **Sit to stand exercise** This is a good basic place to start building the arm strength and coordination to climb the rope. Place sets of 5 up/down reps in with a pushing movement like pushups and a short run. **Anchoring** Establish a strong anchor while sitting down. Sitting on a high box in front of the rope while holding it works on proper foot anchoring on the rope and using your legs and hips to stand up on the rope. These are great to include into a workout that is lower body intensive. It will allow you to learn to anchor the rope while fatigued. One of the hardest rope climbs I have done was at the top of a 3000m climb to the top of Mt. Killington. **Crunch Tuck** Practice a reverse Crunch (bring knees to chest) while hanging on the rope. This is a great exercise for athletes that can anchor the rope but lack the core strength to get to the second pull on the rope. **Coming down** Learn and utilize a proper "J"-hook technique. This helps get down the rope quickly as it creates a pulley system using the feet and legs on the way down. Sometimes I run into athletes that can get up a rope but have problems coming down the rope. Be sure to practice being efficient on the way down. This will help save some energy and you will have a lot of confidence on the rope.

Race Day	The rope in the race is usually smaller than most climbing ropes in gyms and certainly muddier! Good strong anchoring is going to be the best way to get up the rope. Your arms will also be tired and worn out so the more you can use your stronger, more resilient legs the better off you will be.
Coach Notes	Use the legs and hips properly, try not to climb with the arms too much. Once your legs are anchored push with your legs and squeeze your glutes while climbing your hands up the rope. Your legs should be straight and your hips flat at the top. Be sure to practice often so you do not forget the technique at the race. Yes, I have done this early on in my racing days and have seen others stare at the rope with a confused look. You get to the rope after a long hill climb and completely forget what foot or technique to use. Therefore, you must practice often but also under some fatigue.

Obstacle	Slip wall
Description	An 8' 45 deg incline wall that is smooth with a rope hanging halfway down
Training	The best training you can do is to find a 45 deg incline you can practice running up while keeping your form and core tight.
Race Day	Short quick steps are best. Do not try to 'jump" or reach for the rope too soon. Be patient and try to run past the rope or top.
Coach Notes	Most people just do not train proper incline running for this obstacle. They usually are running too fast and leaning too far into the wall or looking down instead of up.

Beware getting your weight too far ahead of your feet. If you get on your toes too much and your weight is too far forward your feet will slip out from beneath you. Most athletes also reach too early for the rope or top of the wall. This creates the same issue of having your body weight too far in front of your feet. |

Obstacle	Cargo Net – A frame
Description	A 45-degree cargo net climb and descent pprox.. 20' high in an "A" formation
Training	A-frame cargo net climb is best trained by working on proper contra-lateral bear crawls. Meaning when you do your bear crawls you really focus on the opposite hand and foot moving at the same time. Work on forward and backwards bear crawls at a moderate or slow place with your knees just 1-2" off the ground. This will build the correct motor pattern, coordination, agility and stamina needed for the A-Frame climb.
Race Day	In the race I always go close to the side or where the supports are. The net is firmer and less bouncy. I line the vertical seam of the net up with the middle of my body. So instead of looking through the net I am focusing on the seam of the net and grabbing the horizontal seams. Having a good motor pattern will allow you to move confidently and allow your body to do the movement you have practiced so you do not have to think about it. A crucial point for those that might be afraid of the height, if you focus on the movement and not the result it can be easier.
Coach Notes	The A-Frame is a tall structure at the races. This can cause some issues for athletes that are afraid of heights. I suggest focusing your eyes on the webbing and not the ground. Focus on moving at an even and controlled pace. It can be helpful to have a teammate in front or behind you to help you stay calm and keep moving.

Obstacle	Cargo Net – Vertical
Description	A cargo net that is attached high and hangs down vertically like a wall.
Training	The Vertical Cargo net is very similar to climbing a ladder. The vertical cargo net height can range from 8-10 ft attached to a horizontal wire to a mega structure of 15-20+ ft. that goes up and over a vertical staging structure or wall. The basic training for this if you do not have a net is contralateral bear crawls. This movement shares the same climbing pattern to go up and over the net. The most challenging part for most athletes is transitioning over the top, especially if the netting is loose or it is a wire instead of aluminum staging. If the netting is losing your feet will push the net forward past the top secure point. This makes it difficult to use your legs to get over the wall and you must rely on your arms to pull your body over the top. Get your chest over the wire first or lay across the wire. Then pass your legs over. There are fancy/faster/riskier ways to get over the top. This usually involves grabbing the netting on the other side and flipping or rolling over and hanging on the net. This can sometimes lead to your feet getting caught or losing your grip and falling. This advanced move takes practice in a safe environment with a soft-landing pad.
Race Day	Try to climb the net close to secure and stable points like the anchors or edges of the net. There will be less sway and bounce from other racers climbing.
Coach Notes	Most issues with this obstacle happen towards the top transition or on the way down. Work on feeling the sway and bounce of the netting. Work on getting your chest over the top and feeling secure before you get your legs over to the other side. Secure your feet and then start climbing down

Obstacle	Sternum crusher
Description	A large log approximately 2 feet in diameter that is raised 4' of the ground that you must get over.
Training	Work on vaulting over stacked up mats or boxes. Start with a surface above hip height with your hands on top and jump up to a straight arm position and support your body weight. Then work on jumping, support and get a leg on top and transitioning over. Strong triceps will help the support position and working on vertical leap (jumping high) will help you get on top of the log.
Race Day	In a race, slow down and walk up to the log. If it is low enough, place your hands on top and jump up and lay over the log. Then swing your legs over. If it is higher at about chest height you may need a bit of acrobatics. Take your strong hand (for me that is my right) and place it on top. You will need to simultaneously jump, pull your chest to the top of the log and swing your right leg up (you will now be sideways) and roll-on top of the log hugging it with your arms and legs. Be careful getting off the other side. Make sure the ground is clear. Since the log is round, you will need to push yourself away when getting off to keep your legs from swinging under and you sliding down onto your back side.
Coach Notes	Do not run at the log thinking that horizontal speed will help with vertical jump. A running start does not really help get over this obstacle. If anything, it reduces your ability to jump up and get on top of the log. I had a race partner do this and crack a rib by hitting it too hard.

Traversing Obstacles

These are obstacles that you must cross in a horizontal or lateral manner. This could be moving sideways across a rock-climbing wall, across a log or hanging from a rope that you must go across upside down. These obstacles usually require good grip and arm strength. Some require some forethought to make it across.

Obstacle	Z-Wall
Description	The z wall is a horizontal bouldering obstacle made up of 3 walls angled in a "Z" formation. 2x4" blocks of wood are attached that you need to step and grab onto while moving horizontally across and around corners to hit a bell. Each wall is approximately 8' wide. You cannot touch the ground.
Training	Finger, hand and forearm strength is a big part of this obstacle. I suggest working on movements that would strengthen the grip. Towel pull ups, Farmers carries with heavy dumbbells or kettlebells (for an added training option use a towel through the kettlebell handles), Pinch grip plate carries, and deadlifts are all good movements to add to your training. You will also need shoulder strength to hold your body up. Add in dead hangs for time (work up to a 1 min hang). Something else I see on the course is athletes have their hips too far away from the wall. Really try to keep the hips close to the wall. Turn out your toes so they are pointing in opposite directions. This will require external rotation of the hips. I suggest working on the frog stretch in your warmups to open the hips up.
Race Day	Two things have really helped me be successful on this obstacle are 1) the way I place my hands, and 2) which wall and direction the wall is facing. Hand placement, I like to "cup my hands and place them on the outside edges of the blocks rather than grab the blocks on the front with my fingers. This outside placement allows me to stay close to the wall and "swing" a bit. I place my hands and then shuffle, step my feet over, then move my hands again. I know I am right-handed so I lead with my right side. I search for the least used and least muddy wall facing in the direction I want to go. I also check out the grade of the slope and make sure the wall isn't leaning too much to my side.
Coach Notes	Placement is key for this obstacle. Make sure that you are gripping with the hands correctly and your hips can get close to the wall. The way to fall off is having your weight far away from the wall. Have your weight pulled towards the ground.

Obstacle	Tyrolean traverse
Description	A thick rope or cable strung across water or suspended horizontally above the ground for 30-50 feet. You must traverse the rope without touching the ground. This is done by hanging under the rope or laying on top of the rope.
Training	If you do not have a long rope, you can use I have found that slacklines can be a good alternative to practice with. They can be set up easily between two trees and stored easier. You are also very likely to know someone that has one versus a 50-foot rope. The only downside is that they are bouncy and have a slight edge to them. Wear thick pants or sweatpants when trying this. In the gym, I work on good static core strength. Planks, bird dogs, reverse crunches, Knees to elbows and Russian twists are all great movements for developing the core strength needed for the Tyrolean traverse. If you have a long pull up bar or tree branch work on going from a dead hang to pulling your legs up to the bar or branch and wrapping your legs around it and then coming down under control. Alternate which leg wraps around the bar or branch first.
Race Day	In a race the ropes may be muddy and/or wet. Do your best to scope out a clean rope. Look at the bow to the rope as well. If you are tall (< 6') there may be a chance that you will hit the ground if the rope has stretched. Speed, arm and core strength are your main weapons here. If you are under the rope stay close to the rope and move fast with short arm reaches and quick leg over leg transitions.
Coach Notes	You want to try to keep your chest close to the rope. Many times, I will see an athlete hanging with straight arms. This creates too much distance with the body, and you are limited by your grip strength. If your arms and legs get too straight you will not be able to move and will fall off. If you lose your core (tension in your abs and sides) most of your body weight will start to drift towards the ground. Do your best to keep the arms bent at 90 degrees and the rope at your knees instead of your ankles (I highly suggest long socks and pants for this). Use an alternating hand over hand, leg over leg pattern such as hand/leg/hand/leg. Move quickly, you will have less than 2 mins before your body starts to give out. If possible, get on top and lay across the rope and pull yourself across. It has a much higher chance of success. You can also rest while laying on top of the rope. The one downside is usually a rope burn across your chest and ankle.

Obstacle	Balance beam
Description	A log or length of wood above the ground that you must walk across
Training	Start with a series of 2x4s on the ground, practice walking across wearing your trail running shoes. When you can make it across 8-10ft raise the wood up off the ground 1-2 ft. Most trail running shoes have big lugs that make balancing on a small or round surface difficult. Practice will help, especially when the surfaces are wet and muddy.
Race Day	The race day conditions will play greatly into an obstacle like this. If it is wet and muddy it will be more difficult to make it across the log or plank. Try to remove any excess mud from your shoes if possible.
Coach Notes	Try not to run across the beam. Moving quickly will only speed up any imbalances and not give you time to recover from any mistakes. Make sure you have your balance on one foot before transferring your weight to the next foot.

Obstacle	Log hop
Description	A series of 8-10+ upright logs that are stuck in the ground end up and placed about 3-5 ft apart. They are in a nonlinear pattern to make it more difficult to make it across. Some may even be at different heights.
Training	Practice first with dots or weight plates on the ground in a zig-zag formation. Practice landing on the balls of your feet and absorbing the impact with your legs. Land quietly and surely. Practice swinging your leg to help give you momentum to make it across longer distances. Wear your trail shoes to practice this. Once you feel confident with the movement and the landing you can raise the landing spots up off the ground.
Race Day	Race day conditions will determine a lot of success with this one. The more wet and muddy the conditions the harder landing and balancing will be. Make sure to remove any excess mud from your shoes.
Coach Notes	Try not to run across the pegs. Most designers leave in one or two long gaps that are at an odd angle. If you are moving too fast you cannot change direction fast enough to make a course correction. Also, these pegs are sometimes loose and wobbly creating an unstable surface. If you have too much forward momentum you will not be able to settle your weight onto the peg.

Obstacle	Slackline
Description	A taught cargo line 2" wide approx. 10' in length that the athlete must balance and walk across. The line is usually 6-12" above the ground.
Training	Start first on a 2x4 on the ground and practice centering your balance. Then move up to a proper slackline. Most rock-climbing gyms will have one to practice on. The hardest part is keeping your balance when you step due to the "bounce" in the slackline.
Race Day	The Slackline will be muddy. Take your time and focus on the end. If you try to watch your feet you may shift your weight forward.
Coach Notes	Bending the knees will help to absorb the bounce. Also, do not move too fast as we tend to rotate the torso when we add speed. Keep an even pace as you move forward.

Obstacle	Olympus
Description	A traversing wall that is slanted about 15-20 degrees with multiple styles of hand holds. Short chains, holes, and rock-climbing holds. There are no foot holds
Training	Grip, grip and more grip. Really work on those farmer's walk, pinch carries, and bent hangs or negatives on a pull up bar. If you have access to an angled wall or climbing wall practice hanging and moving laterally. Use a pattern like hand-hand-foot-foot. Practice crossing your hands over each other.
Race Day	This obstacle is the middle point between the grip heavy hanging obstacles, the Z-wall and the slip wall. It is at just enough angle to make it challenging to keep your feet on the wall, especially if it's wet and muddy, and keep your grip. What they also throw at you is various choices of grip. 3 choices is just enough to make you doubt your strategy on how to get through the obstacle. If it is wet and muddy do not go for the chains. They are the most likely grip to be slippery causing you to fall off. The holes are the best and strongest grip to grab. The spacing might be too much for some people so you may need a climbing grip to hole pattern.

Speaking of pattern, figure your hand placement out before you get on the obstacle. You should already know where your hands are going. You will need to keep your hips as far away from the wall as possible to reduce foot slippage. I have seen some athletes successfully use their knees instead of their feet. I personally found this method too painful. |

Coach Notes	The Olympus poses too many options to get across. Racers can sometimes not know what to use or did not decide before getting onto the wall. Poor body position, not enough arm strength, and poor foot contact are usually why racers fail this obstacle. Get a good grip hold and feet as flat on the wall as you can. It is okay for the hips to be far from the wall. This will give your feet some stability. Remember to use three points of contact as you move across the wall. I like to move my hands to a new grip then move my feet. The longer you stay on the obstacle the more likely it will be that you lose your grip.

Obstacle	Ranger Ropes
Description	A ranger rope is a set of 2 ropes that span a hole or are above the ground. One rope is directly above the other about 5 - 7 ft apart. You walk on the bottom and use your hands on the top one to help stabilize as you traverse a gap.
Training	If you can set up two ropes between trees you can practice this move. Work on moving sideways in both directions so you can find a way that feels best for you.
Race Day	The trick with the ranger ropes is to not lean backwards or forwards. The rope or cable on the bottom will push away and you will only be able to support yourself with your arms. Stay centered over the bottom rope and use the top rope to help keep your balance. Core stabilization is key as well as keeping your feet pointed forward and a slight bend in the knees to absorb any shock from the movement. You will want to slide your feet and then your hands.
Coach Notes	Do your best to not stabilize by pushing and pulling with the arms. The arms should be used to gently balance you and your legs to stabilize and move you across. Bending the knees, a bit may help keep the weight pulling down.

Strength Obstacles

These are obstacles that require Power and Strength rather than endurance or speed. These include heavy objects that must be thrown, pulled, carried or picked up. Some may require strength over time and others are explosive and powerful. All rely on a strong body to accomplish.

Obstacle	Hercules Hoist
Description	A strength obstacle, you must lift a weight attached to a rope and pulley into the air approx. 20' and lower it down under control
Training	In training, start by doing seated rope sled pulls. If your gym doesn't have sleds, you can easily replicate this with old tires and a rope. If you can get a pulley and rope system set up, start by lifting light weight and working on proper grip and technique and then add weight. Sometimes the sled or weight can be too light so make sure you start with a weight that gives some resistance.
Race Day	This is one of the few obstacles that I like to use gloves with. A good set of gloves can reduce the chance of rope burn and help grip the thin and muddy rope.
Coach Notes	Use your center of gravity/body weight efficiently to start the first pull. To start the first pull, grab the rope and pull your elbows into your body and sit down at a 45-degree angle. Let the weight of your body pull the weight up. When you sit on the ground, lay back and start pulling the rope hand over hand, sit up and lay back again while pulling the rope hand over hand until the weight is at the top. You can brace one foot against the railing to help keep you grounded. Stay seated on the ground while you slowly lower the weight using the hand over hand method. Do not let the rope slide through your hands. If you are not wearing gloves getting a rope burn on a muddy course could make hanging obstacles impossible but also could cause the wound to get infected.

Obstacle	Tire Drag and Pull (plate drag)
Description	A tire or sled attached to a 20' chain or rope that you need to pull to you and then drag back to its starting position
Training	This obstacle usually comes at a part in the race where you are tired and worn down a bit. Sled or rope pulls should be a part of your training program. They have lots of carry over too many obstacles and help to build strong arms and backs. Practice pulls standing and sitting with just enough weight to give you some resistance and work up the weight gradually. In training, work on fast and slow pulling.
Race Day	During the race I suggest sitting down on the ground instead of standing. Find a lane that looks relatively clear of holes, bumps, or rocks. There is a metal stake that the rope is attached to, placing one foot on the stake to give you something to push against. Lean back and pull fast and repeat until the sled or tire is pulled to the stake. This allows you to use your legs, back and arms to accomplish this obstacle. Grab the sled or tire and walk backwards until the rope is at the end and straight.
Coach Notes	Use your body efficiently. This obstacle can drain quite a bit of energy and over tax your posterior chain. Try to choose a lane that is free of obstructions like rocks or big divots in the ground. Once you get the sled moving keep that momentum going.

Obstacle	Sandbag Carry
Description	Carrying a 30-60# sand filled object 200m - 400m usually up and down a hill. Not always in a straight line
Training	You simply need to be doing weighted carries in your training. I like to program them once a week and usually uphill. I alternate weeks of short sprints (100m - 200m) with longer uphill hikes (400 - 800m). Learn how to carry them efficiently. Proper distribution of weight is important. For pancakes I like to carry them behind my neck on my upper back. This usually taxes my hands and biceps but allows me to distribute the weight across my back. If I am wearing a hydration pack, I can rest the pancake on top to further distribute the weight. A sandbag can be a little different. It's a bit bigger in shape and usually heavier than a pancake. If the terrain is clear and not slippery, I carry it on my right shoulder and try to move quickly. Alternating shoulders as needed. If it is bad terrain, I will bear hug it and keep it close to my center of gravity, so I am not taken off balance by the extra weight. Practice both carry positions in your training. A great exercise to do with sandbags and pancakes is called the Turkish get up. This movement is a great core strengthening movement. It can also help with balance, hip and leg strength. Normally the Get Up is done with a kettlebell but this variation is much more suited to the Spartan racer.
Race Day	When in a race inspect the sandbag or pancake to make sure it is not leaking or ripped. Look at the course and terrain. Are there spots where people are having issues? Mud puddles or rocks? A bottleneck of people? Once you pick up the weight you want to move at a quick but comfortable pace. Any interruption to your movement could cause you to put the weight down which would expend more energy in picking it back up. Stay very mindful of the terrain, this is one of the few places that I have twisted my ankle due to my mind wandering. If you must put down the weight, have a plan to deal with the stopping ahead of time and try to stick to it. I like to have a plan such as a set number of times I can put it down or a spot on the course, for example "I can put it down two times" or "I can put it down at the halfway point". Give yourself a specific rest period like 3 breaths or 30 seconds and stick with it. If you don't have a plan you will tend to rest longer than needed or focus on negative thoughts.

Coach Notes	Attitude goes a long way with this obstacle. It is grueling and long on purpose. Usually just long enough to be very challenging. At some point this may feel like a slow grind, that may be impossible to finish. This is where a healthy positive attitude and mantra can help you get through moving this sandbag over rough terrain. Know it will be over soon and that when you start running again you will feel lighter.

Obstacle	Farmers Carry
Description	Pick up something heavy in each hand, carry 200-400m
Training	Farmers' carries are one of my "go-to" exercises in the gym. I like to incorporate them 1 - 2x per week in different variations to help build grip and carry strength. I suggest different variations of carries such as: short and heavy carries, Long and light carries, Pinch grip carries, different weight in each hand, DB carries, KB carries, Water jug carries, etc. In a race they may use chain handles on logs, Chain drags, or water jug carries. Keep your grip strong but not white knuckled. Learn to walk quickly with good posture. Good posture will distribute the weight through your shoulders, core, hips and legs. Just leaning a few degrees forward will put strain on your lower back. It's better to put the weight down when your posture starts to go. Be sure to stretch your forearms after and if possible, get a sports massage. Excessive grip work can lead to elbow issues if not properly taken care of.
Race Day	Walk as quickly as possible but avoid trying to run. Even if you feel you can run with the weight you will create torque in your core/spine area if you start swaying/rotating
Coach Notes	Do your best to carry the weight and walk quickly but not running. Keep your grip moderate. A hard grip will tax your grip strength too much.

Obstacle	Tire Flip
Description	A tractor tire that is 400# (Men) and 200# (women) that you need to pick up one end and flip over multiple times
Training	To lift a tire properly you will need to use the proper set up. Squat down, keep your hips lower than your shoulders. Take a wide grip and dig your fingers under the tire so your forearms also touch the tire. If you can get your chest into the tire as well. Lean into it and drive through the legs, pushing and lifting the tire up at a 45-degree angle. Once you stand up quickly get a knee into the tire to help continue pushing the tire up. Flip your hands over to a pushing position and push the tire over. You must commit to driving through the tire or you will stall, and it will come back down. This is a quick and powerful movement that does not really have any point at which you can stop, keep the momentum moving up and forward. You can usually find an old tractor tire that you can grab for free if you can haul it away. It usually costs tire shops money to recycle or dispose of them so you may get lucky if you call around and have the means to pick one up.
Race Day	In slippery, muddy terrain this obstacle will be almost impossible if you cannot get good footing to drive into the ground. Make sure you are in a good and solid spot to plant your feet. Put as much of your body in contact with the tire so you are not relying on just grip strength to hold onto the tire.
Coach Notes	The tire flip is not a deadlift. We are not lifting the tire up in a straight line, it is an angle. Use a proper leg drive forward at a 45-degree angle. Keep the core tight as you extend the legs. If the hips rise faster than the tire you will end up rounding your back.

Obstacle	Log Carries
Description	A small to large log that requires one to two racers to lift and carry for a set distance over terrain.
Training	This one is not too hard to train for as most locations have access to wood or logs or even objects like fence posts or rolled up rugs. You can also substitute rocks and stones for this. Find a log or object 2-3 feet in length and 6-12" in diameter. Pick it up and carry it for 15-20 mins. Carry it with your arms or on the shoulders or back. If it is big enough for two people, make sure one person is on each side to keep it even. Communicate often especially when switching shoulders.
Race Day	Commit to carrying the log as far as you can go, and then take it further before you place it down.
Coach Notes	Try not to run too fast and bump into other racers. Be aware of your other racers and try not to rush past them. Sometimes there is a line or no room to get around another person. Practice patience.

Obstacle	Bucket Carry
Description	A gravel filled 5-gallon bucket that must be carried 200-400m
Training	I like to have 1-2 days that have heavy carries in my workout or after. I mix up the carry with large sandbags that I can bear hug and buckets. Work your way up to 75# for 400m carry. Start light and long and add weight and reduce distance over time. (i.e., 50# for 400m vs 100# for 10mx10 rds.)
Race Day	This is one obstacle that I like to wear gloves for. Piling gravel into a bucket with bare hands can really mess them up. Save your hands for all the grip obstacles by wearing gloves to push the gravel into the bucket. Gloves are also beneficial if you hold the bucket under the bottom. The buckets have a small ridge under that digs into your hands and can make grip obstacles more difficult later. Not to mention that it just hurts. The gloves will protect you from this.

Coach Notes	The bucket carry is meant to be a grueling and tiring carry. It's simple but not easy. Commit to finishing the obstacle mentally and you will have a better outlook to the challenge.
	Different arm lengths will have different proper grips on the bucket. The one I like the best is the bear hug method that we teach in the Spartan Obstacle Course Specialist Class. The bucket is held high against the chest, arms wrapped around, one hand is grasping the other wrist. Squeeze in tight using your lats and back muscles. This keeps the bucket off your hip flexors and close to your center of gravity. This will allow you to move quicker and carry longer.
	DO NOT carry the bucket up upright on the shoulder! There is an artery that runs through that area and if the edge of the bucket is pressing into it that could lead to an injury.

Obstacle	Spear Throw
Description	The spear throw is the bane of many Spartan racers. It is a 20-30' throw from behind a barricade often to a target made up of 2-3 bales of hay. Sometimes the target is a smaller 'archery" style foam target
Training	The spear throw in a race can be the shortest obstacle if done properly
	How to hold a spear If there is a line attached to the spear, make sure the line is untangled and free of debris and knots. Have the line over the fence on the obstacle side to avoid stepping on it.
	Use a full hand grip around the shaft. If there is a line on the shaft, have it run from the back through your hand when you grip the spear
	Have strong but not crushing grip of the spear Hold the spear in the middle where it is balanced
	How to establish proper alignment Square up to the target. Have your shoulders, hips, knees and ankles all going forward towards the target.
	When you throw, try not to rotate or turn the point away from the target.

| Training | Many people miss because they change alignment when they pull the spear back to throw. The point turns away, the shoulder opens too far, and the hips turn away. When they turn back to throw, they unintentionally add rotation to the spear and overthrow across the body or spin the spear sideways.

How to aim
A good method of aiming is to use your off hand to point at or slightly above the target to center yourself. Keep the hand pointing at the target. In training work on bringing your throwing hand to your aiming hand. Do your best not to rotate.

How to throw
Throwing a spear should be more like a short football pass, or a dart throw and less like a javelin or baseball.

Release the spear slightly higher than your aim so you have a bit of a parabolic curve to the throw.

Power
Besides aiming and rotation most people under or overpower their throw. Dialing the proper power will take some practice for the distance. In training, start close to a target and take a step back every 10 successful throws until you can make 8-10 successful throws at 25-30 feet from the target.

Throwing with power requires arms, hips and feet to work together.

Shuffle step
Sometimes when we throw, we need more power. If we just, try to throw the spear harder we will overcompensate and throw wildly. Strength often masks inefficiencies in our movement.

In order to add more power to our throw we will add in a few forward shuffle steps. Keep your lead leg forward and quickly shuffle step forward before throwing. Force = Mass * Acceleration, here we are increasing the acceleration of the throw by moving our entire mass which should result in a more forceful throw rather than just relying on our arms and strength. |

Training	**Mental tips** It seems that race designers love to precede the spear throw with a few specific types of obstacles to throw you off. Running up or down a short hill, Strength, or a grip obstacle. Most of these are placed before the spear throw to elevate your heart rate and leave you short of breath or breathing irregularly. This is intentionally done to reduce accuracy. As your heart rate reaches approximately 170 bpm and above your accuracy decreases. You start to lose fine motor skills and can only rely on previously trained gross motor skills. Accuracy at a high heart rate can be trained but most people except military operators do not need this. So significant training must be put into it. This would not be a good use of training time for most racers. The time needed is just not worth it, instead the racer can learn how to breathe properly and how to lower the heart rate quickly and to focus with good form. Taking 30-60 secs to stop, breathe, focus, visualize, aim, and throw will always beat a missed target and 2-3 mins of soul crushing burpees and disappointment. **Alternative throws** Granny or pitchfork throw. This is an underhanded throw and a great alternative if you cannot throw overhead due to injury or shoulder issues. Hold the spear at about waist height, put your dominant throwing hand on the butt of the spear. Place your lead hand under the spear, extend your lead arm out and cup your fingers to create a channel to guide the spear. Make sure your front hand is straight and pointing the spear just above the target. Use your rear hand to powerfully push the spear through your lead hand and send the spear through the air in an arc. Do not bend your lead/guiding arm. If done correctly the spear will arc up and then down into the target.
Race Day	Accuracy can be highly dependent on heart rate and state of mind. I coach my athletes to slow down and breath before the spear throw. Do not rush into it. Take your time, inspect the equipment. Find a lane where the spear has already successfully hit the target. Visualize making a successful throw. Keep your eye on the center of the target. Throw powerful and straight.

Coach Notes	One of the first things I teach athletes to improve their throwing is to use the non-throwing hand for aiming. Keep it outstretched and pointing at the target.
	When practicing, start without the spear and move your throwing hand from your ear to your aiming hand. You should end up making a triangle with your hands and shoulders. This helps reduce rotation in the throw and keeps everything aligned forward.
	Try to notice how much your hips rotate or if your balance shifts. Most people I see at the races try to throw the spear like a baseball. This usually kicks out their rear leg behind them and gets their center of balance moving forward in front of their body.
	The power for the spear throw should come from the body like a good punch or a dart throw. Push through your rear leg, aim slightly above the target's center and throw forward powerfully in a straight line. Keep your chest and eyes facing the target

Mental Obstacles

Obstacles that require thoughts and memorization instead of physical abilities.

Obstacle	Number memorization
Description	Some races will have a memorization portion. You are given a 9-digit number to remember for an unknown distance. When you reach the checkpoint, you must repeat it exactly or incur a penalty.
Training	There are two popular methods to this obstacle: Chunking and Alpha-numeric phrasing. Chunking requires you to break the number into smaller "chunks" to help you remember it.
	This is the idea behind breaking up a phone number to remember it easier. The Alpha numeric way is to make a memorable word or phrase out of the numbers using corresponding letters.
Race Day	Stay relaxed, positive and confident. Do your best to move the number to long term memory storage. Heightened anxiety or stress will hamper your ability to do so.
Coach Notes	Do your best to not write the number down. Have a plan ahead of time as to how you are going to chunk the numbers or remember them. I like to make a song of the numbers to the beat of my running pace.

12

MOBILITY

Photo: Spartan Media team

Obstacle Course Racing is a tough and demanding sport. As such there are bound to be muscular and joint issues that come up in training and racing. This section is not intended to diagnose or fix any issues but to cover some of the common issues that arise with racers. We will also include some info on self-care and mobility you can do in training and on race day to avoid serious injury.

The topic of SMR (Self Myofascial Release), mobility and flexibility could (and does) fill entire books on their own. Here, we will keep the topics to the essential areas pertaining to OCR only and highly recommend researching more on your own or talking to a Physical Therapist if you have lingering issues.

The most common issues for OCR athletes tend to be foot, shin, knee, hip, forearm and shoulder issues. Most of these issues tend to be preexisting and correctable before getting on the racecourse. We will tackle some easy strategies to help avoid future issues while also giving some tactics to explore existing or persistent issues. Add these into your warmups and training routines to avoid injuries during training or on the racecourse. As always, use your head and discuss with your doctor or physical therapist before attempting any corrections on existing issues.

Mobility Tools

The mobility tools you will need to take care of your body and recover. These tools have become more popular and easier to get over the last few years as education on mobility has become more widespread and not just for physical therapy.

- Foam Roller - A cylinder made of foam or composite material that aids in massaging muscles and moving blood through tissue
- Lacrosse ball or trigger point ball – A hard ball that can help pinpoint smaller areas to create pressure or massage between bones or hard to reach areas,

- A stretch band or large rubber gym band – A rubber band that is 3-5' in length and either in a loop or a single length.
- A barbell or hard roller – Advanced methods may require a hard surface roller such as the end of a barbell or metal roller.

Mobility Tests

Mobility can be described as the ability to move a joint through its full range of motion without obstruction or compensation. Below are a few mobility tests that you can test and then retest to see if your daily mobility is working. They will help you determine if you need to work on your ROM (Range of Motion) to lessen the probability of injuries while completing obstacles. This is not an exhaustive list, and these are just a starting point. Please consult a PT or doctor if you find you have issues.

Overhead Reach

Hanging obstacles require a great deal of movement in the joints of the arm. Brachiation (swinging by the arms) requires a full range of motion of the shoulder joint and core support. If an athlete has trouble getting their arm fully straight overhead, with their bicep by the ear, we can expect some issues to start to develop. Use this test to determine if your overhead position needs work.

Test:

- Stand with your back, shoulders and heels against a flat wall
- Hands down by your side
- Rib cage down, not flared up

With your back against the wall and body straight, raise your arms out in front of you with thumbs up. From the shoulder continue raising your arms trying to get your thumbs to touch the wall above your shoulders without releasing your tight core. If you must arch your back to get your thumbs to the wall you may have something blocking the ROM.

Suggested Mobility:

While laying down on the ground, place a long foam roller under your shoulders, with your arms straight up and down to the ground. Keep your hips on the ground and core tight. If you have trouble getting your biceps by your ears you can add weight to your hands such as a kettlebell or holding onto an empty barbell that is on the ground. This will help facilitate the stretch.

Shoulder Rotation

Test:

With your back against the wall, arms down and your core tight, start by sliding your elbows up the wall until they are at 90 degrees. Keep your shoulders and elbows on the wall and rotate your arms up until the back of your hands touch the wall.

Suggested Mobility:

PVC Pass through - using a 1" PVC pipe that is 6' in length. Hold the pipe with a wide grip in front of your hips. With elbows locked raise the pvc in front and then over your head. Continue behind your back until the pvc reaches your hips. Then reverse and pull the pvc back over your head and to the front of the hips. If you do not feel a stretch, you can slowly move your hands towards each other to narrow the grip and increase the stretch in the shoulders and chest.

Ankle Flexion

Test:

Standing in front of a wall, place your toes against the wall, while keeping your heel on the ground push your knee forward to gently touch the wall. If you can keep your heel down, move your foot back an inch away from the wall and try again. The goal is to have the front of the big toe 3-4" from the wall and still be able to touch your knee to the wall with the heel down.

Suggested Mobility:

If you cannot keep your heel down and touch your knee to the wall you can work on stretching out the calf with heel drops on a stair. Place your toes on a stair and let your heels hang off and drop down below the stair. You should feel a stretch in your calves.

Hip Rotation

Test:

90/90 internal/external hip joint rotation

Sit on the ground with legs in front. Move one leg behind to make a 90-degree angle. Bend the front leg to a 90-degree angle with the outside of the leg on the ground and the shin perpendicular to the body.

While keeping the core tight, bend forward from the hips without bending the spine then come back up to neutral. If you feel you cannot stay in an upright neutral position, and you are tilting to the side you may need to work on your external rotation. If you cannot keep your front knee on the ground, you may need to work on external rotation.

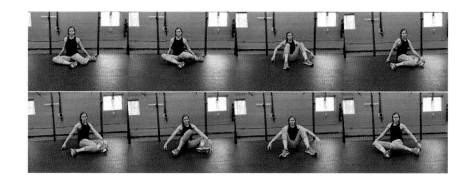

Suggested Mobility:

Internal rotation:

figure four - laying on your back, bend your legs and have your feet flat on the ground. Take your right leg and cross it over the left so your right ankle is at the left knee. Reach your arms under the right ankle and grab behind your left thigh. You may need to sit up to do this. Lay back down pulling the knee towards your chest. You should feel a stretch in the right glute. Hold for :30s then repeat on the other side.

Raised half pigeon on a bench - Cross your leg over the top of a bench or raised flat surface that is about knee height with the outside of the shin lying flat on top of the bench. Place hands on the bench for stability. Slide your other leg back and lower your body towards the floor by bending the rear knee until you feel a stretch. Hold for :30s and then repeat on the other side.

External rotation:

Test:

90/90 hip switch rotations

This is the same as the 90/90 test above except that you start with a small range of motion and increase the range over a few weeks until you can get both knees to touch the floor in each direction. Alternate going side to side with a slight pause at each end range. As you become more flexible that range will increase.

Daily Mobility:

Having a daily mobility routine can bring many benefits besides increased range of motion in muscles and joints. Having a wake up and bedtime routine based on moving the body can help rejuvenate you as well as calm you down before bedtime. It should be easy and a bit mindless, so you do not need to over think the movements. Save the complex stuff for your workouts or mid-day stretches.

Full body joint circles

Starting from the bottom joints and working your way up, rotate 5 times to the left and right for each joint area. If doing this at night start from the top and work down.

- Ankles - Point toe into the ground and make circles with your heels
- Knees - Put feet and knees together, hands on the knees, make circles with knees, keep heels on the ground
- Hips - Hands on your hips, feet under hips or together, move your hips in a circle around the center of your feet.

- Torso/lower back - Feet shoulder width apart, keep feet planted, rotate your body at the hips, rotate to look behind you then rotate to the other side.
- Shoulders - Arms by your side hanging down, move just the shoulders up, back, down and forward making a circle motion.
- Wrist - Hands out in front of you rotate at just the wrist down and around and then the other direction.
- Neck - Standing erect drop your chin to your chest, rotate your head towards your shoulder, then back towards your spine, then other shoulder, and back to chest.

Cool Down Yoga Flow

A simple but effective yoga flow that helps develop flexibility but also helps the body cool down after a workout or a long day. Set a timer for 1 min at first and as you get comfortable increase by :30s -:60s until you can do 3-5 mins of this flow. Take your time at each position, feel the stretch then move to the next position. Continue through the flow at your own pace until time is up.

- Downward Facing Dog
- Upward Facing Dog
- Child's Pose

Pre-Workout Mobility

Before doing a workout, it is best to add in some stretches or mobility movements that can help increase your performance and reduce injuries. Here are some stretches and movements that will help increase the effectiveness of your warmups. Add these to your warmup routine.

Downward Facing Dog

This is a beginner yoga move that has great benefits to all athletes. It will help hips and ankle mobility as well as low back and hamstring flexibility.

- Start in a plank position, push your hips up and back while pushing your head and shoulders between your arms
- Heel should push down to the ground and arms and hands are pressing into the floor.

Scorpion Stretch

The scorpion stretch is a great thoracic rotation stretch that will increase flexibility and mobility in the hip flexors, core and shoulders.

- Start by lying face down on the floor, stretch your arms out to the side and legs straight.
- Take your foot and reach across your back towards the opposite side of your hand. Try to keep the shoulders on the ground or close to it. Repeat on the opposite side.

Wipers

- Lift both feet vertical to the sky/ceiling
- Lower to the side together trying to keep the shoulders pinned to the ground.
- If needed this is easier to do with bent knees and the legs at 90 degrees.

Iron Cross

- Lift one leg up to the sky with the sole of the foot facing the sky or ceiling. Keep your shoulders against the floor. Lower the leg across your body (if the left leg is up it will fall to the right side of your body).
- Lower it as far as you can keep your shoulders pinned to the floor
- Bring the leg up back to vertical and switch legs, repeat with the other leg in the other direction.
- You can add a strap or rubber band to the vertical foot to help keep control and tension on the hamstring as well as help guide the leg.

T-Spine stretch

The T-Spine stretch is an Iron cross variation. Instead of having the legs straight you will bend both at the knee and waist to 90 degrees. With shoulders on the floor lower both knees to one side parallel to the floor, Grab the top leg at the knee and pull it towards the chest and grasp the bottom leg's foot or ankle and will pull back/up towards the shoulder. The legs should look like they are making a sideways "S" shape. Try to keep shoulders close to the ground.

**The wiper, iron cross and t-spine stretches are similar. The wiper is with both feet together and the iron cross/T-spine are one leg at a time. All start by laying on your back with arms stretched out to the side and palms down on the ground.

Running Mobility

Runners tend to just jump up and go without any warmup or stretching. While you may be able to get running without any prep work, I would like you to slow down and spend some time stretching before and after your runs. You do not need to spend a lot of time stretching but just enough, so your body is ready to move. On the days you are not running go through some joint mobility to check in on your body and get a diagnostic check.

Here are some areas of flexibility and mobility that are often overlooked by runners. In trail running you need your feet to be flexible enough to conform to the terrain and debris on the trail. The big toe plays a huge role in balance and forward movement. Taking care of the foot and big toe will reduce ankle and foot injuries and help maintain performance. Climbing a hill or wall is very difficult with an injured or immobile big toe. Excessive running and training for longer races will impact this area. Make this part of your daily routine

Arch

Tool Needed: Lacrosse Ball

This is a great way to help relieve the symptoms of Plantar Fasciitis or tight arches. While standing or sitting, place the lacrosse ball on the bottom of the foot. Add pressure by shifting your weight onto the ball. Start at the heel and move side to side while working the ball up to the front of the foot where the toes start. Then work your way back down. Repeat 3-5x or as needed. Then work the ball front to back. Roll your foot forward and backward while applying pressure.

Big Toe Rotation

- Sit down on the floor and cross your legs and grab your big toe with the same side hand. Manipulate the toe by making circles with it and pressing it up and down for a stretch.
- Do this 5 times on each toe in each direction.
- Push down the big toe towards the bottom of the foot. Give slight resistance (push back) from the toe. Alternate with pushing the toe up (towards the ankle) and giving some slight resistance in the opposite direction. This will help stretch the toes stabilizing muscles.

Ankle Mobility

Ankle mobility is very important in squatting, climbing, and running. Flexion (pulling toes closer to the shin) is needed in uphill running, wall climbing, and squatting down. Extension (toes pointing down/away from shin) is used for pushing off, running, sprinting, jumping, balancing. Lateral (side to side) mobility helps reduce ankle injuries like rolling the ankle or any lateral falling.

Ankle Circles

While sitting on the floor, Grab the foot with the opposite hand and above the ankle with the same side hand. Manually rotate the foot/ankle in circles 3-5x each direction. Push on top of the foot where the toes/foot meet to stretch out the top ankle. Push the foot to try and rotate the foot inward (towards the arch) to get a more lateral outside of ankle stretch.

Ankle Lateral Stretch

This ankle side stretch helps reduce injuries from rolling your ankle while running. Start standing and barefoot, you may need to hold onto something for balance. Shift your weight to one foot, the other foot you will "roll" to the outside, this will stretch the side of your foot and ankle. Hold for 10-20 seconds then shift to the other foot.

Couch Stretch

This stretch is for the hip flexors and the quadricep muscles. Both play a big role in running and climbing over obstacles. You will need a wall or bench for this.

- From a kneeling position place your knee on the floor close to the wall and the top of your foot against the wall. Your shin should be parallel to the wall. You may need a soft mat under your knee.

- Step forward with your other leg into a lunge position. Sit up straight slowly. Just go as upright as you can, do not force it. The goal is to get your back/shoulders to the wall. For a deeper stretch you can raise one arm at a time overhead to the wall.

Pigeon/Glute Stretch

Running uphill, jumping over things and scrambling over rocks and debris take its toll on the glutes. This is an area most runners ignore until they start to develop IT band issues.

- Start sitting on the ground, back upright. Cross one leg in front so the inside of your leg is facing up and push the other leg straight back, so your knee is on the ground. Place your hands on the floor by your knee and foot. Lower your chest towards your front leg. Go slow and try to get your chest to your leg.

- This can also be done raised off the floor placing your front leg sideways on a bench or box. Straighten out the back leg and lower the knee towards the ground until you feel a stretch in the side of the glutes.

Obstacle Mobility

Climbing over, under and through obstacles takes its toll on the body. If you can move well and fluidly you will reduce the risk of injuries while training or racing. On the course you may run, jump, crawl, and climb through various scenarios. Just an inch of greater mobility in some areas can be the difference between completing an obstacle or receiving an injury.

Lower Body

- **Getting Low**

Crawling under barbed wire or through tubes requires you to get low to the ground. Most people I see on their first race have their hips too high in the air for most obstacles. This could be because of lack of proprioception awareness (i.e., where their body is in space) or a lack of ability to lower their hips or knees close to the ground.

- **Deep Squat**

With your feet just slightly wider than your hips, sit down to as low a squat as you can get. Pick your chest up so your back is straight. For a deeper stretch place your elbows inside your knees and apply light pressure to push the knees away from each other. If you have trouble getting into this position some weight may help. Hold a dumbbell or kettlebell close to your chest to help weigh you down. An alternative is using a 10-15# weight plate and hold it at arm's length from your chest. This will help you keep your back straight.

- **3 Position Lunge stretch**

The 3-position lunge stretch is an excellent hip opening movement and hip flexor stretch. I was taught this one by my buddy, Coach Todd Cambio. I was really surprised how it opened me up and how good it made my hips feel. When trail running your hips are constantly adjusting in all directions. This stretch really helps the hips joints.

- Start in a lunge position, Right leg forward, foot flat on the ground and knee at 90 degrees, rear leg back, knee on the ground, this is position 01. Once you are in the lunge position start the stretch by pushing your knee forward over your toes. Keep your chest up and shoulders over your hips. Return to the lunge position.
- Take your front foot and move it away from your centerline about 45 degrees to the side. Keep your centerline (chest and spine) facing forward, only your leg moves. This is position 02. Shift your knee forward over your toes on that leg. Only go as far as is comfortable. Return to center.
- Next move the foot out again another 45 degrees. Your legs should now make a 180-degree angle. This is position 03. Keep your centerline facing forward as in position 01. Shift your knee over the toes. Only go as far as is comfortable. Return to center.
- Now switch legs and repeat on the other side.

- **Groiners**

These are a great hip mobility and stretch for getting over and under obstacles. It is like a lunge but goes farther in the stretch. A prerequisite to climbing objects is the ability to get your knee to your chest. Use this stretch to increase that mobility.

- Start in a plank position with arms straight.
- Take one foot and step to your same side hand. You should now be in a lunge position with your hands on the ground. For a deeper stretch try to place the same side elbow on the floor. Hold this position for 10-30 seconds then switch sides.

- **Frog Stretch**

    This is another great deep hip stretch. This one is great to gain flexibility for climbing over walls and under obstacles. This one can be uncomfortable on the knees if it is a bare floor. I suggest placing mats or pads under the knees for this one.

    - Start in a kneeling position on the floor, hands on the ground in front of the knees.
    - Move the knees away from each other, spreading them as wide as you are comfortable. Rotate your feet out so the arches are on the ground.
    - Start the stretch by sitting the hips back and towards the ground. As soon as you feel a stretch or discomfort stop the movement.
    - Move the hips forward and toward the ground. You may have to walk your hands forward as well. Stop when you reach the ground, feel the stretch or any discomfort.
    - Continue rocking back and forth very slowly and pausing at the front and back to feel the stretch. Move the feet/knees wider if needed.

Upper Body

- **Forearms**

Due to the pulling and hanging nature of OCR obstacles racers may develop golfers or tennis elbow. This is when the ligaments, tendons and muscles of the forearm that are near the elbow become inflamed and holding objects can hurt. We want to add in some mobility work to lessen the chances of this occurring.

- **Finger Push Stretch**
  - Put your hand in the center of your chest with the forearm perpendicular to your body.
  - Push your fingertips towards your elbow. You can do 1, 2 or all 4 of them at a time. I prefer 2 at a time

- **Wall/Box stretch**

This stretch helps the shoulders open. You can use a waist high box or a wall for this stretch.

  - Place hands on the top of the box or against a wall. At or greater than shoulder width. Feel free to move them closer if needed.
  - With your legs straight, push your hips back and push your head and chest through your arms. Your body should make a right angle at the hips, and you should feel a stretch through the shoulders.

- **Towel Wringers**
  - Starting in a standing position move your feet out wider than your hips and put your arms out straight to the side. You should now be in a "star" looking position.
  - Turn one hand up rotating from the shoulder so the whole arm turns. Rotate the other arm from the shoulder, turning the thumb to the ground then behind you. Your arms will feel like you are "wringing" a towel.

- Lean your head towards the hand that is facing up, you should feel a stretch in the neck and shoulder. Lean to the other arm and rotate the arms in the opposite direction. Hold this position for 5-10 seconds before alternating back to the other side. Do 4-6 reps in each direction.

- **KB Halos**

This is a great shoulder rotation to warm up and stretch. You will need a light kettlebell for this. You can use something like a plate or ball, but the kettlebell works best.

- Hold the kettlebell upside down by holding the "horns" or sides of the handle.
- Keep the kettlebell close to your chest, start by moving the KB to the side of your head, then behind the head, and then to the other side.
- Do this circle around the head as a fluid movement in both directions. The KB should not be so heavy you cannot move well. Repeat 5 circles in each direction.

13

NUTRITION

Photo: A.dEntremont

Training and racing nutrition is a huge subject and can be a book of its own. I am not a nutritionist or registered dietitian. To get guidance specifically for you please seek out a qualified professional.

In this section I will detail some anecdotal findings based on my personal accounts and results from my athletes. It will also be kept simple and geared towards the newer racer. Most of this will be what you need to know before getting to the start line and you will have to test and tweak your nutrition out during your training.

One of the biggest pieces of advice I can give is to not change anything on race day. There are usually lots of giveaways from companies at the races. It's possible that the free protein bar giveaway may not agree with your stomach. Wait until after the race to try anything new.

Hydration

Hydration is not just simply taking in liquids. It includes water and electrolytes. A hydration plan and system are essential if your race is longer than 5 miles. I have been in long races where they ran out of water to give out (There was an issue with a water well and the delivery system to the top of a mountain).

Proper water rationing can make or break your experience during a race. Even though in this book we are focusing on the shorter races, understanding your hydration needs can help you have great training runs and adjust properly due to different weather conditions.

It is important to know your sweat rate and how much water you need to ingest during your runs. This also helps you determine how much you need to carry, how to adjust for heat/humidity, and what supplements you may need to have with you.

Hydration strategy should all be addressed and tested during your training runs and should be dialed in about 3 weeks from the race. I believe that even in low water situations I have been mentally prepared due to training in some of these harsher conditions safely and educating myself as to how much I need for what distances and how far I can go on just water and not supplementation. This takes some trial and error as well as preparation.

Water Intake

Drink to thirst - Your body is smart about when it needs water. There are telltale signs that you need to take in water. This should become evident during training such as salt rings on your clothes and around your mouth, fatigue levels and cramping. These signs usually mean that we need to take in more water for similar runs in the future. Rather than trying to force yourself to drink on a specific schedule try to drink to thirst, when you are thirsty drink, and monitor how much you have in relation to how far or long you must go. Below we will go over the sweat rate. This will help you figure out how much and possibly when you should be drinking by testing and calculating.

How Much Should You Drink?

Should you drink more or less? Most runners or athletes do not take this into account during their training or during a race. Luckily, it's simple to get a general answer. The simple method is to weigh yourself before a 1-hour training run and weigh yourself after. If you lose weight, drink more. If you gain weight, drink less. If it is hot or humid, drink more. This calculation is a very simplistic way to do this. There is a more complicated and scientific method to do this that may be out of the scope of this book.

To keep track of how much you drink most running bottles or hydration bladders will list the volume. Simply mark where the liquid level is when you start and when you finish. Please note that outside temperatures, elevation and terrain will play a role in changing your sweat rate. The hotter it is the more you will lose. You will also lose more electrolytes during warmer weather. Increasing electrolyte or just sodium intake during warmer temperatures can be beneficial. If you are hiking vs running on flat terrain you will need to take into account, the elevation gains over time as well as the starting and ending elevation. More elevation will require more fluids.

Electrolytes

- **What are electrolytes?**

Electrolytes are essential to the operation of the human body and can be depleted through sweating, urine or overhydration. These essential minerals are Sodium, Potassium, Chloride, Calcium, Magnesium, Phosphate, and Bicarbonate.

Eating a solid healthy diet will get most if not all of these into our system normally. Electrolytes help regulate our body's pH balance, muscle contraction, electricity/nervous system and more in our body. When we exercise, we lose electrolytes through sweat and urine so we must replace them before we lose too much.

We can replace them on the racecourse by putting them in our water supply or carrying an extra bottle with an electrolyte solution. The number of electrolytes lost while sweating will vary from person to person so testing your dosage is needed. Most people will be fine with moderate intake during or after if the event is under 90 mins unless the temperature or humidity is high.

- **Why do I need them?**

Electrolytes are needed to do a whole lot in the system but in an endurance event they help regulate fatigue and cramping. When you are depleted of electrolytes you may start to get headaches, cramping, fatigue, muscle twitching, and some may feel that their heart is racing.

- **Supplementation Sources**

There are a host of companies on the market that are eager to help you supplement your training with electrolyte chews, goo's, liquids and tablets. Some of these are fantastic and others simply have way too much sugar in them. Be careful to read the labels and reviews of these products.

Some of these products may not agree with your system so please test them out on training runs. If your run is less than 90 mins a mixture of water and electrolytes will be fine. Find a delivery system that will work for you. Powders and tablets are the easiest to get into a bottle or hydration bladder.

Race Day Nutrition

For races that are less than 90 mins in length our race day nutrition does not need to be complicated. Have a good breakfast in the morning about 1-2 hours before the race starts. If you are travelling for the race from a hotel or driving, eat when you get up but prepare some food to eat about 45-60 mins before the start.

• Short Race vs Long Race Nutrition

A quick chat about nutrition and distances. As we increase distance from short 5k/10k (< 90mins) races to longer ½ marathon to marathon distances (>2 hrs.) we also need to change how we think about our nutrition strategies.

In the shorter races most, daily nutrition will get us through a race that is less than 90 mins. Some food or a meal 45 mins before should be sufficient. In longer races over 90 mins athletes will need to think about adding calories in the form of drink or food. Longer mountain races will require you to take in an extra 100-200 calories per hour to sustain your output. You can add calories to your water through supplements or keep gels and chews on you to add simple sugars and calories.

In longer races/training runs you will want to start consuming calories and electrolytes before you will need them. This may take some trial and error to find something that agrees with your digestive system as well as timing of when to take them and how much.

Never change your nutrition strategy on race day.

Please read that again. This is non-negotiable. Changing or diverting from your normal foods can cause numerous issues and unintended consequences. At best it will cause digestive issues. At worst you may have to leave the race altogether without finishing.

14

STAYING INJURY FREE

Photo: A. Oulette

During a race there are many injuries that are avoidable. Most of the time they can be avoided if the racer is shown a few basic rules or techniques to keep in mind during the race. The main factors that contribute to the injuries are overconfidence, lack of knowledge or awareness, and fatigue. This is where proper training for the race can impart a great awareness of your body and surroundings during the race.

When our heart rate passes 115-120 bpm, we start to lose fine motor skills, at approximately 150 bpm we lose complex motor skills, develop tunnel vision and lose the higher cognitive abilities (i.e., good judgement, interpreting depth perception) that help keep us safe.

However, we may see an increase in Gross, trained motor skills at 150 bpm. Which means that you can only use what you have trained using. At about 175 bpm or above we start to have a breakdown of motor skills. In longer races this is important to understand as you may not be going fast but your heart rate may be up, and you are most likely fatigued.

Most injuries that I have witnessed tend to be to the ankles and knees. Most are obtained while tripping or dropping off a wall or high object. Unfortunately, most racers do not spend enough time developing flexible, strong ankles and feet. As well as not having enough upper body strength to climb down/off a tall obstacle, thereby leaving it up to their legs to take the impact of the fall.

They usually have no problem getting up the obstacle but are either fatigued by the effort it took to scale the obstacle or lack the knowledge/ awareness of how to get off the obstacle, sometimes this is technique and sometimes fear can cause you to freeze on top of a high obstacle. This usually results in them hanging and jumping/falling off into the mud which could be hiding rocks/debris and cause a sprained ankle or in one case I witnessed, a buckled/dislocated knee and another time a tib/fib fracture w/ bone protrusion.

Reducing injuries during a race

First, slow down before an obstacle. If your heart is beating fast (<170 bpm) your fine motor skills are not accessible, this is how small avoidable mistakes are made. Take a few seconds to LOOK and ASSESS the obstacle before jumping into it.

Analyze

Come up with a quick plan and path to success, envision it, then tackle it with confidence. If you have to think in the middle of an obstacle, you will not react quick enough and will waste energy.

Choose the most efficient way over/under/through with the least amount of energy spent. The most efficient and safe way may be a few seconds slower. Remember the saying "Slow is smooth, and smooth is fast", just a few moments of critical thinking or proper setup will save you from lots of frustration and may be the difference between a successful obstacle or burpees. Look at the obstacle, find one that was completed successfully already if possible.

Make sure the obstacle lines up properly and is not missing equipment. I was once on a hanging obstacle high over water and was about to complete it when I got to the last hanging ball on a rope only to find out the last ball had come off. I slipped right down the rope and into the water with a burned hand and 30 burpees to do.

Lastly, look before you land. Check the ground/mud before you drop off an obstacle. Mud and water can hide rocks and roots. What if the person that went before you did not look and was injured? It would be possible for you to land on them injuring both of you. "Look before you leap".

Cramping

Cramping in a race can be a very shocking and demoralizing event for an athlete. It can be avoided and trained for with some education. The longer the race or time on your feet the more likely cramping can occur from running. In an OCR, cramping can also come from localized fatigue due to some obstacles that require certain movements such as jumping during a wall climb.

Cramping is believed to be caused by lack of water and electrolytes (electrolytes include sodium (Na+), potassium (K+), calcium (Ca2+), bicarbonate (HCO3-), magnesium (Mg2+), chloride (Cl-), and hydrogen phosphate (HPO42-)).

Some things to keep in mind about cramping:

Cramping is not primarily caused by loss of electrolytes in most if not all athlete cases. If that was the case the whole body would seize up not just an isolated muscle group which is what we usually see happen

Salt intake is not always the answer. Most cramping in the studies stopped well before the salt or salty substance could get into the athlete's system. Leading some researchers to believe that it's the "salty" taste on the tongue that starts the relieving of cramps. Pickle Juice is a great example of this.

Most cramping is neuromuscular so water CAN be helpful, but hydration levels seemed to make little to no difference on cramping in some studies.

Massaging the muscles reduced the cramping faster than Sodium or electrolyte ingestion. Stimulating the Muscles (and activating the Golgi tendon) reduced the time a muscle cramped.

Regular massages on the affected area can help reduce the frequency of cramping.

Pre-Fatigue. Cramping is possibly related to protection of an area before injury occurs. Some studies cited examples of former trauma (or over training) to an area and the muscles started cramping to protect it from further damage. It could also be an area of low conditioning for that muscle group or being subjected to a different training stimulus for that group.

Most beginner athletes that cramp is really undertrained for the environment they are racing in especially when it comes to hilly or mountainous terrain. Higher frequency of elevation training (total ascent/descent) is needed in most athletes. If an athlete is training for a race that has hills or mountains, they need to train more on a steep slope and for longer distances. This could be in the form of hiking or running. Occasionally wear a vest or carry a heavy sandbag. Calves and quads cramp the most so make sure those body parts are getting higher volume training over time as well as lots of mobility work.

Hypothermia

In obstacle course races you will often be going in and out of water and running while wet. If you have a drop in body temperature this could result in hypothermia. It is important to tell your teammates if you are having trouble warming your body up. Every race has emergency crew out on the course to help in cases like this and will drive you off the course to the medical tent.

If you are running on a mountain, check the weather at the base and the top of the mountain. Running raincoats and survival blankets are light and easy to pack for longer races. You would rather have them and not need them than need them and not have them. Be sure you know the signs of hypothermia:

- Shivering
- Slurred speech or mumbling
- Slow, shallow breathing
- Weak pulse
- Clumsiness or lack of coordination
- Drowsiness or very low energy
- Confusion or memory loss
- Loss of consciousness

If you or a teammate start to experience these symptoms immediately try to warm up and seek medical help.

15

TRAINING PROGRAMS

Photo: R. Borgatti, Athletes: E. Pomegas, M. Pomegas, B. Stumpf

In this section I will include different types of training programs. Some are specific and inclusive, meaning they are meant to be followed as written as they include running, obstacles and conditioning. Others are specific to the topics or weaknesses of athletes such as grip work, speed work or overall strength. I have also included specific OCR style workouts for athletes that feel they have a good training program and want to just add a few unique workouts into the mix.

Short Distance (3.1M/5k)

Race Example: Spartan Sprint

6 WEEK - 5K OCR PROGRAM

This program was written with the beginner to intermediate racer in mind. A person that has some gym experience or maybe has already run a race or two but had difficulty during the race.

This program will consist of 3 days of training 2 strength and conditioning days with obstacle work and 1 Aerobic day.

If you have more than 7 weeks until the Obstacle Race focus on walking/jogging/running for 20-30 mins 3 times a week and starting a flexibility/mobility routine each day.

Start this program 7 weeks out from a race.

On the days that you are not working out, focus on flexibility and mobility. Spend at least 20 mins stretching and use a foam roller for 10 mins on your lower body and back.

The main goal for this program is to get you fit for an obstacle race. The workouts are designed to give you a wide breadth of strength and skill to be able to tackle any obstacles and finish a 5k obstacle race with confidence.

Terminology:
- Distances are done in meters or "m", 400m = ¼ mile
- Weights are often written in pairs such as (30/20#) this means 30 pounds for bigger athletes or males, 20# for smaller athletes or females.

- Any modifications that can be made to the workouts will be written below the workouts. Some workouts may have multiple weights listed like this (20/10#) if you are a beginner, please choose the lighter weight option or if you are familiar with the movement and want a challenge choose the heavier weight.

Terms:

- AMRAP = As Many Rounds (or Reps) As Possible, when written with a number it means to continue as a circuit without rest for that time (Ex AMRAP 10 = As many rounds as possible for 10 mins). Once you complete the round of work you start over again at the beginning until the time limit elapses.
- WK X/Day X Modifications = Each workout will list substitutions and modifications for challenging movements.

Equipment you will need for this program:

- A gym where you can run and lift, most CrossFit gyms will work for this. If you do not have access to a gym almost all workouts can be done with minimal equipment or minor substitutions.
- A place to run. A treadmill can be used but access to an outdoor running area is best. All long runs should be done on a trail if possible.
- A timer, stopwatch, or clock
- A rope to climb, 10-15'
- A wall or tall object to climb, 4-7'
- Boxes: 8-24" for step ups and box jumps
- Weights: Dumbbells, Kettlebells, Sandbags, 5-gallon Bucket, Pull up bar, Spear, Slam Ball

Aerobic work:

All Day 3 aerobic work was written with track distances in mind as most people will have access to a school track or a treadmill. Ideally, we would like this to be done on a trail or fire road if possible, to simulate race conditions. If you do have a trail to run on, please make sure that you are familiar with it and mark off or note your distances on the trail for accuracy before you do the Day 3 runs.

Cardio substitutes and conversions:

In the program we commonly list running as the main mode of aerobic work. Sometimes this is not always an option due to weather, equipment or injury. You can substitute any running part of a workout for rowing or biking. You can also convert the distance to an estimated time to complete. This is best for those new to working out or that have been out of it for a bit. Do what you can in the time suggested. Here is a conversion chart that will help:

RUN	ROW	BIKE	TIME
200m	250m	.25M	1min
400m	500m	.5M	2min
600m	750m	1M	3min
800m	1000m	1.5M	4min

m = meters

M = Miles

400m = .25M

800m = .5M

Warmup

Do this before every training session.

The warmup is meant to get your body temperature up and get you ready to move well. We use a dynamic style warm up to get you ready for the workout, start off easy and not too fast. Feel free to add any specific stretching needs to your routine after the dynamic warm up.

Dynamic Warm up:

200m Jog

then x20 reps each

- Jumping Jacks (clap hand behind back and overhead)

- Cossack Squat

- Mountain Climbers (L&R=1)

- Air Squats

- Lunges

- Burpees

200m Jog

WEEK 1

Day 1

Hang Hold Test

This test is a Max Effort Hang hold from a pull up bar.

Time how long you can support your body hanging from a pull up bar.

You will retest this in week 6.

Form tips: Keep ears away from shoulders and core engaged.

Test Results:

Beginner :30+

Intermediate :45s

Advanced 1 min+

2 min Rest

FIT Test

This is a test of muscular endurance. We use the simple movement, the Burpee, to test your level of endurance. This is a repeatable test. As your level of fitness goes up so should your burpee count.

You will retest this in week 6.

AMRAP 5 min Burpees

As many Burpees as you can do in 5 mins

Test Results:

Beginner 30

Intermediate 40

Advanced 50+

5 mins Rest

Then

Conditioning

AMRAP 20 mins

10 Ball Slams (25/20#)

10 Walking Lunges

10 Sit ups

200m Run

Rest 1:00

Wk. 1/Day 1 Modifications:

- Burpees: If burpees are a challenge, you can substitute a movement we call Up/Downs, It is a burpee without the push up or jump.
- Lunges: any variation of lunges can be performed. You can do the lunges in place, reverse step, walking or for a challenge jumping lunges. If you cannot do any lunges substitute box step ups or squats with your heels raised on a small weight plate.
- Slam Ball: If no access to a slam ball you can substitute squat jumps
- Run: You can substitute any cardio movement for the run. Most common is rowing or biking instead of running. Use the conversion chart above.

Day 2

Crawls

4x :20 work / :40 rests each movement, then do the next

These are best done outside on grass but can be done in the gym.

Bear crawl

Crab Crawl

Army Crawl

Conditioning

5x

200m Sandbag run/walk (30/20#)

10m Bear Crawl

10m Crab walk

10 Lunges

10 Burpees

Wk. 1/Day 2 Modifications

- Crawls: If you do not have a 10-20m run for crawls you can do a shorter version by moving a few steps forward and a few steps backwards. Such as one, two steps forwards and then one, two steps backward.

Day 3

Aerobic Work

6x400m jog/run

Walk 400m between runs

Each run should be slightly faster than the last if possible.

For beginners a sustained pace is more important

Should be able to talk while moving.

If you are not recovering enough to go again in 2-3 mins you are going too hard.

WEEK 2

Day 1

Pull ups

    5x5

    Adv.: Towel pull ups

Obstacle practice

5x Wall climb (~6')

1:00 rest between

Work on efficient movement

Conditioning

AMRAP 20 min

20m Bear Crawl

10 Step Over Box Burpees (20"/12")*

20 Walking Lunges

1 Wall Climb (6-7')

400m Run/walk

*Do a burpee then step up and over a box, that is 1 rep

Wk. 2/Day 1 Modifications:

- Pull ups: If you cannot perform pull ups substitute recline rows or TRX/Ring rows. If you do not have access to any suspension trainers like a TRX swap the movement with dumbbell rows
- Wall Climb: if you do not have access to a wall or anything like a wall that you can climb over then find something that is above waist height (3-5') that you can climb onto or over. If the object is below 5' double the reps. If you are outside, it can be any type of platform or area that you can climb on such as a retaining wall or loading dock. In the gym you can stack sturdy boxes on top of each other. Please make sure they are secured and stable. Some gyms even have a rock-climbing wall. Please use your discretion and be smart and safe when climbing. If you do not have anything to climb on like a wall do 3-5 pull ups or bar muscle ups.

Day 2

Push ups

    5x5

Spear Throw

    10:00 practice spear throw

Start close to target (~10') and each successful throw move back 5' to a maximum of 25' from target

Conditioning

5x

200m Farmers Carry (35/25 KB)

10 Burpee Pull ups

200m run

10 KB swing

10 Push up

Cool Down

400m jog

5:00 Practice spear throw

400m jog

Wk. 2/Day 2 Modifications:

- Pushups: If you cannot do a push up or have trouble with them there are a few variations that you can do.
- Incline pushups: place your hands on an object above the floor like the wall, a bench or a box. Start easy and as you progress with this movement you can lower your hands closer to the ground
- Knee Pushups: start by laying on the ground. Pick your feet up off the ground but keep your knees on the ground. Place your hands beside your chest with elbows facing behind you. Keep your core tight. Press your hands into the ground and start the push up. As you go upkeep your body in a straight line, do not bend at the hips. At the top your hands, knees and shoulders should make a triangle. Lower your body back to the ground.

- Spear Throw: a spear can be any long straight stick that you can throw like a spear at a target. It is easy to build your own spear from plans on the internet.

Day 3

Aerobic Work

5x600m jog/run

Do 10 burpees after each run

Walk 400m between sets

WEEK 3

Day 1

Dumbbell Presses

5x10, increase weight each set

Rope Climb

Practice rope climbing and descending

3-5 ascents of 10-15'

Practice J-Hook and S-wrap methods

Conditioning

AMRAP 20

100m Sandbag Incline walk/Jog (Hill) (50/35#)

10 Burpees

10 Box step ups (24/20")

100m Farmers Walk (53/35 each hand)

Cool Down

400m jog

Wk. 3/Day 1 Modifications:

- Rope Climb: start off with practicing the different anchoring methods of climbing the rope. Once you can anchor properly and stay on the rope, move to pulling yourself off the ground from a seated position. Then combine the two by climbing the rope in 2 pulls then 3 pulls up the rope.
- Sandbag Walk/Jog: The weights listed as race standards 50# for men and 35# for women. Choose a weight that you feel is appropriate from 10-50#. If you do not have a sandbag, then carry anything you can walk quickly or jog with. Some substitutions are a weight plate, dumbbell, or weight vest. Try to do this on an incline surface or hill. If you do not have a hill, double the distance.

Day 2

Dumbbell Deadlift

5x10, Increase Weight each set

Rest 1:00 between sets

Heavy Carries

8x 1:00 work / 1 min rest

Load up a bucket or bear hug a heavy sandbag and walk

If loading a bucket start light and increase to 70/50#

Conditioning

AMRAP 20

400m Run

100m Bucket Carry (35/25# or 50% of above carry)

10 Pull ups

10 Burpees

Wk. 3/Day 2 Modifications

- Run: Reduce run if 400m takes longer than 5 mins, we want to be in the 3-4min range or faster.
- Heavy Carries: This is a front-loaded carry. Using a 5-gallon bucket load up to race weights which are 70# men and 45-50# women. You can use sand, plates, gravel etc. This can be challenging on the grip, core and low back. Lower weight if problems arise. In the conditioning workout lower weight by 50% of heaviest carried.
- Pull ups: If you do not have access to a pull up bar or cannot yet do pull ups substitute a recline row, ring row or heavy dumbbell row.
- Burpees: These burpees should be quick. If you feel slow cut reps in half (5) or do up/downs (no push up or jump)

Day 3

Aerobic Work

4x800m

Walk 400m between runs

Cool down

Jog 1 Mile

WEEK 4

Day 1

Dumbbell Push press

5x12, increase weight each set

Rest 1 min between sets

Monkey Bar Practice

8:00 practice on monkey bars

If you do not have access to Monkey bars

Do:

8x :20 work/ :40 rest

Quick alternating hand release grip on pull up bar

Conditioning

5x

400m Run

5 Burpee Pull ups

20 KB Swing (53/35)

20 Overhead Plate Lunges (45/25# plate)

200m Farmers Walk (53/35)

Wk. 4/Day 1 Modifications:

- Burpee Pull ups: The burpee pull up is a burpee into a jumping pull up. The burpee portion can be changed to an up/down (a burpee without the push up). If you do not yet have pull ups the pull up bar should be between eye level and top of your head. If you have a few pull ups the bar should be slightly above your head. More advanced athletes will have the bar height between their wrist and 6" above their fingertips
- Kettlebell Swing: If you do not know how to do a kettlebell swing, please find someone that can coach you through learning it. Substitute kettlebell swings with dumbbell deadlifts.
- Farmer's Walk/Carry: This is fast walking holding onto something heavy. Pick a weight that walking 200m will be challenging but doable. Aim for only putting the weights down once or not at all in the 200m.

Day 2

Dumbbell Hang Power Clean

5x8, increase weight each set

Rest 1:00 between sets

Obstacle Practice

5x easy pace

200m jog

1 spear throw

1 rope or wall climb

Rest as needed, do not go to fatigue

Conditioning

5x fast pace

100m Sandbag run (50/35#)

10 Slam balls

10 Push ups

10 Walking lunges

Cool down

1 Mile jog

Wk. 4/Day 2 Modifications:

- Dumbbell Hang Power Clean: This can be a challenging move for some. If you find the coordination for this movement difficult then substitute for dumbbell hammer curls. A Hammer curl brings the dumbbell from your side up to your shoulder with your thumb on top. Do not rotate the dumbbell so your palm turns into your shoulder.

Day 3

Aerobic work

60 min jog

Every 15 mins stop and do 5-10 burpees, including at the start and end of the 60 mins

WEEK 5

Day 1

Overhead Hold

Hold a barbell, dumbbells or sandbag overhead with arms locked out

8x :30s Hold / :30s Rest

Adjust weight up/down as needed to be challenging

Conditioning

AMRAP 30

800m run

100m Farmers Carry (53/35)

10 Box Jumps (24/20")

2x Wall climb (6'/4')

Wk. 5/Day 1 Modifications:
- Overhead Hold: If the first round of :30s holds is challenging with a light weight then lower the hold time down to :20s.
- Box Jumps: Jump onto the box and step down. Choose a height that you can comfortably jump onto the box for 10 reps. This height will be different for each athlete. Listen to your gut. Most people will get butterflies in their stomach or hesitate if the box is too high for them. If you do not want to do box jumps you can do plate jumps (jump onto a weight plate) or tuck jumps (jump and lift your knees up). Also, if needed drop the reps from 10 to 8.

Day 2

Renegade Row

5x10 (5L/5R)

Rest 1 min between sets

Increase weight as needed

Obstacle Work

Alternating Bar or Ring hold

10x :20 work / :40s rest

Alternate each min

Active hang, arms extended

Chin over bar/ring hold

Conditioning

AMRAP 20

400m run

20 Walking lunges

20 Push ups

2 Rope climb (12/10')

Cool down

1 mile jog

Wk. 5/Day 2 Modifications:

- Renegade Row: If rowing from the plank position is difficult switch to a bench supported row. Place the opposite side hand and knee on a bench during the rows.

Day 3

    Aerobic Work

    5K run/jog

    Note time to complete

    Adv: do 30 burpees immediately after

Wk. 5/Day 3 Modifications:
- Burpees can be Up Downs
- 5K can be walk/jog/run

WEEK 6

Day 1

    Hold Re-Test

    Max Effort Hang hold

    Hang from pull up bar

    (Goal = 1 min+)

    2 min Rest

    FIT Test

    AMRAP 5 min Burpees

    (Goal = L1: 30, L2: 40, L3: 50+)

    Rest 5 mins

    Conditioning

    "Mini OCR"

    AMRAP 30

    400m Run

    1 Wall Climb

400m Run

100m Bucket Carry (50/30)

400m Run

Rope Climb (15/10')

400m Run

1 Spear Throw

30 Burpees

Cont. from beginning

Rest as needed, go at a sustainable pace

Wk. 6/Day 1 Modifications:
- Can reduce time to 20 mins
- Run can be reduced to 300m
- Bucket carry can reduce weight
- Rope climb can be rope sit to stands
- Burpees can be Up Downs

Day 2

Alternate Hold/Pull

8x :20s work / :40s rest

Overhead hold (Barbell/DB/Sandbag)

Max Pull ups (record reps)

Weighted Box Step ups

AMRAP 5 mins

Do as many step ups as possible in 5 mins

Wear a weight vest, carry a sandbag or hold dumbbells (50/35#), (16/12" Box)

Goal: 24 steps/min for men (120 steps) and 22 steps/min for women (110 steps)

Conditioning

Re-test workout 1

AMRAP 20 mins

10 Ball Slams (30/25/20)

10 Walking Lunges

10 Sit ups

200m Run

Rest 1:00

Cool Down

1 Mile jog

Wk. 5/Day 3 Modifications:

Pull ups can be ring rows

Ball slams can be plate Ground to Overhead

Walking Lunges can be Step ups

Day 3

Aerobic Work

4 Mile run

Every Mile stop and do 20 burpees

Wk. 5/Day 3 Modifications:

Can walk/Jog/Run

WEEK 7

Taper week

Day 1 & 2

Easy jog 45-60 mins

Stretch

Day 3

Race Day!

Moderate Distance (6.2M/10k)

10k Transition Program

8 Week Running Program w/ Speed work

10k race Ex: Spartan Super

This running and bodyweight program is meant to help bridge the gap between the 5k and 10k race distances. After completing the 5K program you can move onto this one. I do not have any obstacle training here specifically because it was done in the 5k program. If you want to continue training obstacles you can add in a 1x week session.

WEEK 1

Day 1

1M Time trial (Track)

This is a test. Go as hard as you can

Warm up for 20 mins before attempting

Record your Max HR

Day 2

  30 burpees

  Then

  2M Road or trail; Easy pace

  Then

  20 Burpees

Day 3

  4M Trail; Easy Conversational Pace

  60-70% Max HR or below 170 BPM

WEEK 2

Day 1

  4x1 Mile Repeats (Track)

  Rest 1:1

  Start slow, get faster each Mile

  Then

  3 rds.

    20 burpees

    20m bear crawl

Day 2

  3M Road or trail

  Easy - Moderate pace

  do 10 burpees every mile

  2 rds.

    20 Burpee pull ups

    20 walking lunges

Day 3

5M Trail

Easy; 60-70% Max HR or below 170 BPM

15-20 mins stretching

WEEK 3

Day 1

6x800m repeats (Track)

1:1 rest

Start slow, get faster each set

Adv: do 10-30 Burpees after each repeat

2 rds.

30 Walking Lunges

15 push ups

Day 2

30 Burpees

Then

3M Road or trail

Moderate pace; Run hard on hills,

Alternate fast and slow every 15 mins

Then

30 burpees

Day 3

6M Trail

Easy - Moderate pace

Alternate fast/slow every 15 mins

Monitor HR, try to maintain consistent HR for fast/slow portions (ex 140 slow 60%,180 fast 80%)

WEEK 4

Day 1

Hill sprints

4x400M (Road or Trail)

Find a hill

Carry 20 - 40# Sandbag walk/jog or run

10 - 20 Burpees at the top of hill

Day 2

5M Road or trail

Tempo - Fast/Hard

Mile 1: Slow

Mile 2: Moderate

Mile 3-4: Hard

Mile 5: Slow

Day 3

7M Trail

Easy; 60-70% Max HR or below 170 BPM

20 mins stretching

WEEK 5

Day 1

8x200m Sprints (Track)

20 walking lunges between sprints

Start slow, go faster each set

Day 2

    5M Road or trail

    Easy Pace

    Hill Sprints

    4x200m sprints up hill

    30 burpees

Day 3

    8M Trail

    Easy, Conversational Pace

    60-70% Max HR or below 170 BPM

WEEK 6

Day 1

    1M Time trial (Track)

    This is a test. Go as hard as you can

    Warm up for 20 mins before attempting

Day 2

    4M Trail

    Moderate-Race Pace

Day 3

    6M Trail

    Easy Pace; 60-70% Max HR or below 170 BPM

WEEK 7

Day 1

    1M Recovery Run on Road or Trail

    Easy pace; Feel Good

Day 2

    2M Trail

    Easy pace; Feel Good

Day 3

    5M Trail

    Moderate Pace; Feel Good

    Wear racing clothes

    Test out nutrition and gear.

WEEK 8

Day 1

    2M Road

    Easy pace; Feel Good

Day 2

    1M Road Easy

    Recovery; 50-60% Max HR or below 160 BPM

Day 3

    Day before race

    1M Easy Pace; Feel Good

Speed Track Program

    This program is 1x week speed work. This program is aimed at athletes that are okay or even good runners that want to increase their speed and improve cadence and stride. The cadence pacing is meant to help create awareness of foot turnover while running and shorten the length of your stride, so you move faster and improve your running form.

    To do cadence work you will need a wearable metronome or an app on your phone that can work as a metronome. A metronome is a device to keep accurate beats. Musicians use them to keep in proper time. Runners can use them to keep proper pace. By training with one you will learn how to keep your speed. A metronome will beep at a specific interval such as 180 beats per minute. For running I like to set it to half (90 bpm) so it beeps only on my right foot. You will need to try it out to see whether you like it to beep on one or two footfalls.

    The average runner runs at 165 steps per minute. The ideal pace to get the most elastic benefit is 180 steps per minute. You may need to adjust the program up or down in cadence a few steps depending on your ability and experience.

    Use the first week's cadence work to help set the starting point for you and adjust for each week from here. If you cannot maintain form or speed on a particular day, drop back to a pace you can maintain. Once you are comfortable at that cadence move onto the next faster cadence.

    Start each session off with the same warm up drills to help set the proper running form needed.

Warm Up Drills:

    400m jog

    100m jog backwards

    then

    2x each drill (20m jog between sets back to start)

    a) 10 Chicken walks/Reach

b) 20 Bunny Hops w/ forward lean

c) 20 Static alternating foot pulls leaning on a wall or fence

d) 20 Moving foot pulls, Alt side every 10 steps

e) 20 Marching high kicks

Cadence/Speed Work:

Week 1

1x each drill

Rest :90s between sets

a) 1x100m @ 70 (140 steps/min)

b) 1x100m @ 75 (150 steps/min)

c) 1x100m @ 80 (160 steps/min)

d) 1x100m @ 85 (170 steps/min)

e) 1x400m @ 80 cadence

Rest 5 mins

d) 1 mile Baseline Test (4 laps of track)

Week 2

1x each drill

Rest 2 mins between sets

a) 1x100m @ 70 (140 steps/min)

b) 1x100m @ 80 (160 steps/min)

c) 1x200m @ 80 (160 steps/min)

d) 1x200m @ 85 (170 steps/min)

e) 1x600m @ 70-80 cadence

Rest 5 mins

f) 4x200m

walk 200m back to start

Week 3

1x each drill

Rest 3:00 between set

a) 1x200m @ 75 (150 steps/min)

b) 1x200m @ 80 (160 steps/min)

c) 1x200m @ 85 (170 steps/min)

d) 1x200m @ 90 (180 steps/min)

e) 1x800m @ 80-85 cadence

Rest 5 mins

f) 6x200m

Walk 200m back to start

Week 4

1x each drill

Rest 4:00 between sets

a) 1x300m @ 80 (160 steps/min)

b) 1x300m @ 85 (170 steps/min)

c) 1x300m @ 90 (180 steps/min)

d) 1x400m @ 90 (180 steps/min)

e) 1x800m @ 90 cadence

Rest 5:00

f) 4x400m

Walk 400m between sets

Week 5

1x each drill

Rest 4:30 between sets

a) 1x300m @ 85 (170 steps/min)

b) 1x300m @ 90 (180 steps/min)

c) 1x400m @ 90 (180 steps/min)

d) 1x600m @ 90 (180 steps/min)

e) 1x800m @ 90 cadence

Rest 5 mins

f) 3x800m

Walk 400m between sets

Week 6

1x each drill

Rest 5:00 between sets

a) 1x400m @ 90 (180 steps/min)

b) 1x400m @ 95 (190 steps/min)

c) 1x400m @ 100 (200 steps/min)

d) 1x400m @ 100 (200 steps/min)

e) 1x800m @ 90 cadence

Rest 5 Mins

f) 1M run re-test

Then jog 800m cool down

16

INDIVIDUAL WORKOUTS

Photo: R. Borgatti, Athlete: D. McManus

In this section there are individual workouts that you can add into your routine. Use them as benchmarks, tests or just to add a change to your existing routine. I have named these workouts based on the feeling they gave me when testing them out. The workouts use terms you may not be familiar with so I will describe them now.

Results: The result levels are a good guide to workout intensity options. I suggest that you start as a beginner and only progress to doing the workout at the next level if you can complete the previous level. This means it may take you doing the workout 2-3 different times over the course of a few weeks or even months to progress to the next level.

Some levels list suggested weights such as 50/35, This usually denotes a male/female suggested weight loading. These are just suggestions for guidance. Most workouts should be loaded around 50-70% of a 1 rep max load. Start at the lightest load and progress up over time based on your ability.

AMRAP = As Many Rounds (or Reps) As Possible

In the given time domain (ex: AMRAP 20 = 20 minutes) repeat the circuit, score is how many complete rounds + extra reps you got in the allotted time.

EMOM = Every minute on the Minute

Do the work in the time allotted and rest until the next round starts. EX: EMOM for 10 minutes do - 10 push-ups. This means on a running 10-minute clock you do 10 push-ups within 1 min and rest the remaining time until the next minute starts. Sometimes this can be written as "E1M for 10 minutes" where the 1 can be any number of minutes to perform the work such as E2M or E5M.

All Out = 90-100% effort for the duration of time

This is just as it sounds, do not hold back and give all you have for that time period.

OCR Fitness Benchmark Tests

Testing is an important part of training. Without it we won't have objective data on whether we are improving, plateaued or declining in performance. Below is a set of tests that can be done at the beginning and end of a training cycle. You can stack multiple tests in a single training session if there is enough rest to recover. Retest a benchmark test every 6-8 weeks

Test 01: The Spartan FIT test

Most new racers to a Spartan Race should expect to complete 60 - 90 burpees during a race. Most people can get through 2 minutes of burpees before they run out of gas. This test will see where your conditioning and muscular endurance currently is, especially after the first 2 mins.

Test

- How many Burpees can you complete in 5 Minutes.
- Set a clock for 5 minutes, perform as many burpees as possible in that 5 minutes. Have someone else count for you.

Check Your Results

Elite level: 80+ burpees, shoot for 90+ as a goal

Advanced level: 65+ burpees

Intermediate level: 50+ burpees

Beginner level: Under 50 burpees, shoot for 30+ as a goal

Test 02: Max Hang Test

OCR races have lots of grip dependent obstacles. Monkey bars (and variations), rope climbs, carries, pulling, etc.

Test

- How long can you hang on a pull up bar or similar structure?
- Hang from a structure (a pull up bar is ideal). Make sure it is high enough that your feet cannot touch the ground. When you touch the ground, the test has ended. Have someone record your time.
- Results
- Work for a 1–2-minute hang. It is okay to move your hands, let go or shuffle your hands around. If you use chalk, make sure you record that as well. A few of the members of the Spartan Race Pro team have been clocked at 5+ minutes of hanging

Check Your Results

Elite level: 5+ Mins

Advanced level: 3+ mins

Intermediate level: 2 Mins

Beginner level: 1 Min

Test 03: 2 min Burpee Wall Climb

Climbing a wall while fatigued is a skill that can be practiced. This test will help you develop a strategy and show you what breaks down first and what you will need to work on.

Use 4' or 6' walls for this test

Test

- For 2 mins do a burpee in front of the wall, as part of the burpee jump vault or climb over the wall. This is one rep.

Check Your Results

(6' wall/4' wall)

Elite level: 20+/35+

Advanced level: 15+/30+

Intermediate level: 10+/25+

Beginner level: 5+/20+

Test 04: Max Russian KB swing 2 min (53#/35#)

The Kettlebell Swing is an excellent movement that builds posterior (glute, hamstring, low back) power and excellent grip strength, as well as muscular and cardiovascular endurance.

Recommended weights are 53# for men and 35# women.

Test

- Swing a Kettlebell to chest height for 2 mins
- Record reps
- Record how many times you put it down

Check Your Results

Elite level: 60+

Advanced level: 50+

Intermediate level: 40+

Beginner level: Under 30

Test 05: Ruck Pack Test

This test was originally developed by Dr. Brian J. Sharkey, originally for testing fire fighters for the US Forestry Service. This will help you develop speed without running, resilience on your feet and give you resistance and cardiovascular training.

Test

- Carry 45-pound pack three miles in 45 minutes.
- 1st time walk and see how far you get.
- If you fail, increase speed/pace each time you attempt until you finish the 3 miles under 45 mins
- Record fastest time for completing the 3 miles with 45#

Check Your Results

Elite level: 30 mins or less

Advanced level: 35 mins

Intermediate level: 45 Mins

Beginner level: 50 Min

Test 06: Incline Treadmill Test

This test will get you ready for elevation/incline training. Needed for any mountain race or course. You can start off with a walk, then walk/run, then run. This will test your initial capacity and pacing. 10 min mile pace = approx. 1.5M distance on flat terrain. Can you sustain that uphill?

Test

- Set Treadmill at 15% incline x 15 min for max distance
- Record Distance
- Retest and try to get farther by increasing pace

Test 07: Forestry Step Test

This is a US Forestry test developed by Dr. Brian J. Sharkey, originally for testing fire fighters for sustained endurance going uphill. Are your legs, glutes and core strong enough to repeatedly move uphill? Do your quads cramp after hill climbs?

Test

- 5 mins Step up and down
- Step on off a box, 15-16 inches for men, 12-13 inches for women
- Maintain a steady of roughly 90 bpm (Women 22 steps/minute, Men 24 steps/minute)

Check Your Results (women/men)

Elite level: 24/26+

Advanced level: 22/24

Intermediate level: 20/22

Beginner level: 18/20

Test 08: Time Trials, Run Speed Tests

Time trials are recorded speed tests. Your goal is to complete the distance as fast as you can do it. These are maximal tests and should be done under testing conditions. Have a way to record your time, another person is best for this. If doing multiple attempts start slow, rest 2 or 3 times as long as the attempt and build to max speed over 4 sets.

Use a Track, Road, or treadmill. Record what type you are using for re-testing. Mark off your area if needed. Warm up for a min of 20 mins using a dynamic style joint and muscle warm up with some bounding. Avoid long static stretches until after the test. Do each test on a different day

Tests

- 800m
- 1 Mile
- 2 Mile
- Record fastest time, Retest 4-6 weeks.

Check Your Results

Elite level: 2:30/5:00/10:00 or under

Advanced level: 3:30/7:00/14:00

Intermediate level: 4:00/8:00/16:00

Beginner level: 5:00/10:00/20:00

Test 09: Burpee Pull Up Test

This is one of my favorite timed benchmark tests for OCR athletes and is an excellent test of lower and upper body pushing and pulling, Cardio conditioning, stamina and grit.

Most people will encounter 90 - 120 burpees in their first Spartan Race. Beginners can start off by scaling the pull up to a shorter height. Start with a bar that is about as tall as you are and jump so your chin clears that bar. As you get better raise the bar until it is 6 inches above your fingertips overhead. At an advanced or elite level, the bar should be one-foot above reach.

Test

- For time 100 Burpee Pull ups
- Do a burpee by first going to the ground
- Do Push up and stand up.
- Placement of hands and feet are key to stay under the bar. Do your best to place your hands and feet directly under the bar and in line with the supports.
- Jump to a pull up bar, make sure you are looking where the bar is.
- Do a pull up, use the momentum from the jump to help get over the bar.
- Rest as needed
- Record your time for retesting

Check Your Results

Elite level: 11 Mins or less

Advanced level: 13 Mins

Intermediate level: 15 Mins

Beginner level: 20 Mins

OCR Skill Based Workouts

The following are some workouts I designed for my private OCR athletes as tests and benchmarks during their training. I created some athlete experience level scaling suggestions for each workout. Give them a try and post your results online.

Path of Destruction

AMRAP 40

100m Sandbag walk/Jog (Hill up/down) (50/40#)

10 Wall vaults (4' wall, Box, a Park bench, or similar object)

10 Sandbag Ground 2 Shoulder (5L/5R) (50/40#)

100m Farmers Walk (53/35# KB each hand, hill up/down)

Advanced: 40/35, 35/26

Intermediate: 35, 26/20

Beginner: BW, 20

Glory of Sparta

AMRAP 60

400m Run

1 Wall Climb

400m Run

100m Bucket Carry (50/30#)

400m Run

1 Rope Climb (15/10')

400m Run

1 Spear Throw

30 Burpees

Continue from beginning until 60 minutes have elapsed

Score = rounds + reps completed

Advanced: 60 mins

Intermediate: 45 mins

Beginner: 30 mins

Ride and Grind

For Time

50-40-30-20-10

Bike or Rower (Cals)

Pushups

Lunges

Burpees

400m run

Rest as needed

Advanced: 50-40-30-20-10

Intermediate: 40-30-20-10

Beginner: Do 30-20-10

THOR

5 rounds

10 D-Ball Over the Shoulder toss, Alternate L/R shoulders (90/70#)

10 DB Renegade Rows (30/20#)

10 Slam Balls (25/20)

100m D-Ball Ball Carry (90/70#, 50m out/back)

*Rest as needed

D-Ball can also be a Medicine Ball, Atlas stone or Strongman Sandbag

Advanced: D-Ball 70/50, DB 25/15, Slam Ball 20/15

Intermediate: D-Ball 50/30, DB 20/10, Slam Ball 15/10

Beginner: D-Ball 30/20, DB 15/10, Slam Ball 15/10

OCR Anaerobic Workouts

For anaerobic training we utilize a lot of fan bike workouts. These are short fast workouts meant to help work on the explosiveness of obstacles.

These workouts do require some experience and strength to get the full effect. Please feel free to adjust them to your level.

Stepbrothers

    EMOM 12 mins*

    Min 1) 10 Cal Bike

    Min 2) 2-3 Rope Climbs (12'-15')

    Min 3) 1 min Rest

    *Advanced 15 mins, Elite 18 mins

Power Burn

    EMOM 15

    Min 1) 8 Cal Bike or Row

    Min 2) 6 Sandbag cleans (50#)

    Min 3) 4 Pull ups

    If you cannot complete all the work in 40 sec, then drop reps

Burpee Burn

    For Time

    30 Burpees

    35 Cal Bike or Run 400m

    rest 2 mins

    20 Burpees

    25 Cal Bike or run 300m

    rest 1 min

    15 Burpees

    15 Cal Bike or run 200m

    rest :30s

    10 Burpees

10 Cal Bike or run 100m

*Each round is meant to be as fast as possible, rest is built in. Concentrate on HR recovery during the rest. Wear a HR monitor if you have one.

Beep This Bike Test

on Fan Bike, stay on bike for rest period

Have someone else keep track of time

:10s All out / :50s rest

:20s All out / :40s rest

:30s All out / :30s Rest

:40s All out / :20s Rest

:50s All out / :10s Rest

:60s All out / Rest as needed

Score = total Cals accumulated

Athlete Interviews

Athlete: Joshua Fiore

Josh Fiore, an elite OCR athlete, who has an extensive list of podium finishes including 1st place at the 2017 Iceland Ultra World Championship. This interview with Josh is from 2016. Josh has been an OCR competitor Since 2011 and is a member of the Spartan Pro Team.

RB: Can you give us a little background as to how you started in OCRs and ultra-running.

JF: I started in 2011 like most people with Warrior Dash, which was awesome. It was in Amesbury Massachusetts back when they had races out there. It was incredibly muddy. I was literally in my camo gear, my battle dress uniform from when I was in the Army, and it was the worst choice ever. I had big boots and everything and it was thick mud. Absolute worst.

It was the funniest thing in the world, but I was so overdressed and unprepared for it.

After that, I did my first Spartan race and that just knocked me on my butt. That was a learning experience. I thought I was in great shape. Following that, I (did) the Death Race four times. Three summer Death Races, one team Death Race — finished all of them. That was where I learned that I could endure a lot of pain for a long time.

This past year I started really getting into the competitive game. I always did the elite races, but like a lot of other people I wanted to see how well I would do against the best. And then when I started doing that I was like, "Wow, I can actually get really fast." I started running a lot more, and then last year I won a couple of races. Most recent win was second place in the local Blizzard Blast race, which was just a small local race. And then pretty much just been training for ultras and a lot of big races.

RB: You were strong and powerful when you started, but you are so much faster now. How did you make that transition?

JF: It was a huge learning curve for figuring out how to get faster while getting better at running longer distances. I tell everybody that gets into running ... you really must know what works for you. For me, it was learning how to run smart. Around here in Massachusetts we have amazingly fast athletes, especially when it comes to the 5Ks and the world races. These guys are doing 14, 15 minutes in their 5Ks. One of the winners — he was first or second place — I went up to him for advice after the race. Extremely nice guy. And he told me quality over quantity, because at that time I was just running as much as I could. There was not really any aim to it. I was just running.

RB: I think that's what most people do: "I want to get better. I'll run more."

JF: Yes, exactly. While that is true, you do need the quantity, you do need the miles; however, you need to do it smart. My important thing now with my training is one day of slow running. It does not matter how ... You could stop, take pictures, have fun, and just run. It does not matter. Run for three or four hours, but just run. It is called time on your feet. Mixed with that, I do some intervals, such as speed training, some tempo runs and hill training. That has made me a better runner: doing it smart (rather) than just going out there and just doing the miles.

RB: What has been your experience with nutrition? What about cramping or muscle fatigue? What advice do you have?

JF: When I did the Spartan Ultra Beast in Killington last year I was hurting because I was running so fast. My first time was like in the three-hour range, my first lap, and this was a two-lap course.

When you are going that fast it is hard to eat as most people know. On my first lap I had one goo packet and that was it. That was like in four hours I had 200 calories, which is just not enough. My goal now when I do these races is to have the Tailwind, and just have a couple Honey Stinger products, which are like a goo product just more natural. It is just sugars and electrolytes in these products, and then simple honey, which is one of the best things I think to eat simple sugars. And just keep sipping at the Tailwind.

It's great because you're already going to be sipping as long as it's in a camel pack that you have, which I suggest even if you're a slow runner, and there's nothing wrong with that. I have more respect for the people that a race takes many hours to finish than my fellow elite runner that runs it in like 45 minutes. I have so much respect for those people that are on the course that long and they are out there working their butts off to finish.

I would suggest to those people to have a camel pack, even though it is a "sprint course". It could take some people two or three hours to finish one of those courses. Anything over an hour I think you should have some type of camelbak or hydration vest.

Athlete: Mike Downey

Mike and I met in 2013 when he attended an OCR prep class at my gym after having a rough go at his first Spartan Race. We ended up working together for the next 4 years on and off throughout the OCR seasons. Mike was one of my favorites to work with. The training and racing were tough for him, but he kept working towards getting better each year. His determination made me immensely proud of him.

RB: What are your experiences with obstacle course racing, your history and background? What got you into OCRs, and where did your journey lead you? Can you give us a little background as to how you found obstacle course racing and how you started?

MD: How I started was back in 2012 when Spartan was doing their first stadium race at Fenway. Being a big, huge Red Socks fan, I had a couple people convince me, "Just give it a try. Give it a try." I have had people who have done Tough Mudder's in the near past, and they've been trying to get me to do it and until this step I was just not interested but then the whole aspect of it being at Fenway and getting to go up and down to the park. Got me a little bit more kind of, "Let's give it a try and see what it is just for the hell of it." That is kind of what got me started into it all.

RB: Were you doing anything before that?

MD: No, it had been years since I had been to a gym. I do not think I ever ran more than one hundred yards in a decade plus. I really was not a regularly active person. So, it was my first time being actually active in my 30's.

RB: Going from not being active, just living your life to doing this, it is kind of quite a jump and a challenge there. Was there anything that kind of pushed you in that direction?

MD: It was more the aspect of getting to spend a day at Fenway and getting to go to some parts of the park that I had never been to before. That is what got me in the door for the event. I had no physical aspect of it, I did not know anything about obstacle racing up until that point.

RB: Did you train for that at all, or did you just do it?

MD: We did some light running work but there was no strength training. We did not know what we were getting into so we did not know what would need to be done so we just went and winged it and our times, how badly we did, show that we were unprepared.

RB: What would you say your experience was like on that first race? From start to finish, what went through your head?

MD: There were three times I was like, "I'm done, I quit, I want out." I was tapping out like, "this is just not going to happen." It was not a fun experience. It was one of the most miserable days and we ended up finishing dead last in the day. It took us like two and a half hours to do the thing. We failed everything that could be failed. It was a rough afternoon.

RB: What kept you going to the end?

MD: A couple of friends just told me to sit, take a minute. Try to regain your senses, give it a minute and reassess things. And they would say, "Okay just a couple more steps, we'll go to the next section, see what happens." And that just went on and on for the remainder of the race.

RB: Your teammates and your friends really helped move you along to complete the race.

MD: Yes, we all had points where we said, "This is not fun, why are we doing this?" We tried to convince each other to stay in the game and try to finish the race.

RB: After that initial experience what made you come back and do more?

MD: A month or two after we did the race, they announced they were going to do another stadium race in New York the following year and at that point my ego said, "I'm pissed, I finished dead last, I know I can do better. I know I can do better." And I said, "you know, let us give this one more try, let us just show myself I can do better. That was just a difficult day." That is what happened. And we made plans to go to New York the following year.

RB: Did you give yourself time to prepare for that race?

MD: About four months to get a game plan together. It went completely opposite from Fenway. By that point I had already started collaborating with you and getting a lot of knowledge and kind of figuring things out and we did that one which was about twice the length in about half the time. We were a lot stronger and faster on it. It was gratifying knowing I can do better, I dug deep, and I was able to find that next level. I have now done four Spartan Beasts.

RB: Did you get anything out of doing these longer distance races?

MD: So, you can laugh but I found that when you are in the middle of being just so mentally broken, once you are broken down mentally is when your mind just starts seeing things differently. You get to this place where your mind opens, and you see things in a new way. Because you are just so disheveled, your mind needs to wander somewhere to find these new parts of you. The Beast will break you a few times over and each time you get broken you see something new that you have never really understood before or until that point.

RB: How would you describe obstacle course racing to someone who has never done it before?

MD: It depends on the race because each race has its own flavor and its own kind of what it is pushing. I usually just explain there are 5ks and 10ks. You get a little muddy, you are going to get a little wet. There are parts where you are going to be really questioning what you are doing but it's good to see what happens when you put yourself in those spots and just see how you respond mentally and physically to those challenges.

RB: What would you say was challenging about doing the obstacles that are in these races?

MD: For me most of the challenge is especially a lot of the grippy hanging stuff being that I am a bigger person in weight. It is more of a challenge to pull myself over a ten-foot wall or doing monkey bars that go up and down. So, for me that is the most because it requires a lot more grit and grip. A person at 160 pounds doing monkey bars needs a lot less grip than me at 260 pounds needs. So obviously there is some obstacles that my weight helped me carry heavy loads.

RB: What would you say to somebody who does not identify as a runner?

MD: I would tell them not many people can run up a mountain so it ends up being a hiking event and can you power hike? Only those top 20 or 30, they can run up and down the mountains. Most people cannot. For most people, it is grueling, but can you gut out the hike? Even the elites at some point just cannot run. So, you tell yourself, "Okay if even they can't run, these guys are top tier athletes so if I'm having a tough time, at least I know they're suffering too."

RB: In the middle of these races, when you are suffering or going to a dark place, do you have any tricks that help you complete the races?

MD: The dark place is not really in the shorter races in the 5km range but when you hit the 10, 15 km stuff it gets there. For me one thing, I will just shut up, I do not talk for a bit, I kind of just head down, take the pain, just try to grind things out. Or it's possible that you have a great obstacle performance and something that just changes the game for you mentally then it kind of really puts you back into the things. Sometimes it is something stupid, one of the things that I carry with me on big races is bacon jerky. And even if you are having a crappy time, you just get a little whiff of that bacon jerky, it just kind of perks you up a little bit, gives you kind of an "okay" and it helps your head snap back into things. Get back into gear. You can only have so many of those goo's and the gels and stuff before you need something that tastes good. And beef or bacon jerky, that's much better than the goo's, the change in the game comes really quick.

RB: Do you have anything that you want to say to somebody that is either just starting off or thinking about doing an obstacle course race? What advice do you have?

MD: Just do the best work as you can at the gym, get as ready as possible. On race day, go out there, just have fun. Don't set expectations too high to where you're going to put yourself in a failure spot and just kind of have fun. And each race, when you finish the race, learn what you did right, what you did wrong. Take that back to the gym. See how you can fix it, make it better and that way you can make the next time that much better and enjoyable. Keep learning from each experience.

Athlete: Danielle Rosvally

Danielle and her husband Mike became members at my gym in 2016. They joined our OCR program and were a mainstay on our team until they moved out of state. Danielle accomplished much while racing with us. As you will read in her story she did not start as an athlete but has gone on to complete many OCRs as well as an ironman and marathon

RB: Were you an athlete growing up?

DR: In no way, shape, or form was I ever an athlete. I avoided sports of all kinds for most of my childhood, and I was a theater kid, so my parents were very encouraging of the arts. And I was like the fat, pudgy, awkward kid, and was not good at sports, could not find a way to fit in with the crew who did sports, so I avoided them. Intermittently throughout my adult life, I would like to start, go into the gym a couple of days a week, but it was never what I would call a healthy lifestyle habit. It became something that was an obligation. I did not really get into sports and training until I was into my PhD, so well into my twenties, because I just needed something that would make me leave the house. So, I started, and I kind of had it in the back of my head that I wanted to run a 5K as a bucket list item. I had never run before, I hated running, but I was like, "I'm going to try this. I'm going to see if I can do it because I feel like I should be able to do it." So I started a Couch to 5K program and worked really, really hard at it and found out that in conjunction with the PhD, which is just like a grueling mental task, having something that made me leave the house multiple times a week, and go out and get some sunshine, and exercise, it was really, really healthy for me in a lot of different ways besides the usually exercise is healthy for you.

So, I ran my 5K, and the first 5K wound up being a Spartan Sprint because I had had a friend who died of ALS, and he was incredibly involved with a guy named Don Devaney. And so, when Frank died, he sort of made public that his wishes for the people he knew were that we would go out and do something that's scary, as a way to honor him. So, the Spartan Sprint was what I chose. And so, I did it, and Don [Devaney] was there, and it was great. I finished it, and I said, "When do I do this again?" So, it started building from there.

RB: What was it about the Spartan Sprint that was scary?

DR: So, in my mind at the time, a Spartan Race was a real test of endurance, and strength, and all the things that I had been seriously avoiding. And I sort of ... I just wanted to know if I had it in me to do it, and I was scared that I did not. So, a Spartan Race, for those who do not know, is going to be less about running, and more about the obstacles you must do, and the obstacles will break down into basically like climbing over the thing, climb under thing, or carry the thing and you sort of have to go through this distance. A sprint is between three and five miles. That one I think clocked out at like five and a half miles.

Looking back on it, it was not intense as far as Spartan Sprints go because it did not have the elevation that we usually expect from a Spartan, but at the time, it was the most challenging thing I had ever done. So, it was exciting when I got to the finish line and was like, "Oh, I have more in the tank. I could have gone faster, I could have gone harder, I could have gone longer. I wonder how fast, hard, and long I can go." And that sort of made me think about what I can do next, and what can I do to prepare for what is next?

RB: Did that first race change anything else in your life for you?

DR: It made me start to think about the activities I participated in, right? So how can I better prepare to do this, and what do I need to do to be better prepared to do this? The first race did not change anything because I had not hit a mental of a physical limit, so I would say the life changing thing was my first Super where we were out for like six hours because it was in New Jersey on a ski slope. And like six or eight miles, it was closer to eight, and it was raining just buckets the entire time.

We were ankle deep mud, out on the mountain, so long, everything became so much harder because it was wet and covered in mud. And that is where I really hit some limits, and that is when I started to think about things like, "Okay. I hit my physical limit, but I kept going. That is incredible. I wonder if I have more." So, that was more life changing than the first sprint. The first sprint was like a foot in the door, sort of a gentle introduction if there is such a thing in the OCR world.

My first Beast was past my limits. I got off the mountain from my first Beast and cried because of how overwhelmed I was that I had done this thing. But that Super really made me start to think about what limits are. Like I kind of intellectually knew that I had limits, but at the beginning I was really scared to think about what they might be, and even forget surpassing them, just like even meeting them. I did not really have a sense of what my physical potential was. And in a lot of ways through training, we are all still trying to figure out what that physical potential is. We are always assessing our limits or how far we can run, or how fast we can do something. Some people have a better idea of it than others, but for me it has always been about where that line is, and how can I move the needle? For the first year and a half of my journey, this is common, but for the first year and a half, it is not about where the line is, it is about what ballpark does the line live in? You are nowhere near the line or your physical potential. You are on this journey to figure out what town you need to be in to find the ballpark, to find a seat where you need to be. So that first sprint was a marker or compass telling me "Okay, go north."

After that sprint, I got more involved with running. So, I went for a 5K to 10K, and through that process I had to rehab my knees. What really got me involved in training was running with my Husband, he had a terrible time. I realized that if I wanted to run these things with him, I had to find a way to get him involved in some sort of training, which is how we found CrossFit because I sort of knew, "Okay, how do you be better at OCR racing? Well, you do CrossFit." I assumed that they would be related. Turns out they are. But at the time, I was just like, "How do I get him in such a shape that he can go with me when I want to push my limits?" So, getting him in the door really got me in the door, which meant that I was humbled in a new way because suddenly my limits were not related to anybody else. I could chase after my own star. And that was huge.

RB: You've also gone on to do marathons. Most people would say that CrossFit or even OCR are different from a marathon. How did you get all these worlds to fit together?

DR: They are, and they are not. It depends on what your goals are. If your goal is to run a fast marathon, then yes, your CrossFit training is going to be a little bit distracting because everybody will tell you "You are not going to get strong and fast at the same time". It is just not going to happen. If your goals are to figure out what the outward limit of your body and your tolerances are, then I do not think they are distracting at all. You and John told me that first year because the year I ran my first marathon was also the year of my first Beast. And you both told me, "The Beast is going to make you better at running the marathon," and it was true.

So, a marathon is an endurance event, you must get in your long runs, and mentally prepare for it, but to be able to do that, you also need a lot of strength in the legs. Popular articles have been coming out recently in things like Runner's World, and a lot of the running community is starting to recognize that training for a marathon is not just about logging miles.

Training for a marathon is about strengthening the systems that your body needs to be able to run 26.2 miles. And a lot of that strengthening happens in the gym, not on the road.

So, for me, training for a marathon while doing CrossFit was great because it meant that I could do a lot of different things at the same time and never get bored with my training regime, and that is why I like kept the marathon on my calendar so steadily. But a lot of runners, and I hear this all the time like my podcasts, a lot of runners hate Cross-training. They just do not like it. They're like, "I hate it. It is so boring. I don't like weightlifting." And I am like, "You have the wrong Cross-training regime if you hate Cross-training." And so, I think that more people who do CrossFit are more capable of endurance events than they know. And especially if you are doing long Spartan Races, you are capable of a running endurance event no problem. I mean, you must put the training in, but if you are training for a Beast or an Ultra Beast, you can run a marathon. I just cannot emphasize enough that if I can do it, anyone can do it.

RB: What would you say to somebody who is on the fence?

DR: Just try it. Seriously in your mind, commit to four to six weeks of showing up. Because if you show up for yourself and just see what it can do, then you will know.

REFERENCES

Schwellnus MP, Allie S, Derman W, Collins M. Increased running speed and pre-race muscle damage as risk factors for exercise-associated muscle cramps in a 56 km ultra-marathon: a prospective cohort study. Br J Sports Med. 2011;45(14):1132–1136. doi:10.1136/bjsm.2010.082677.\

Miller KC, Stone MS, Huxel KC, Edwards JE. Exercise-Associated Muscle Cramps. Sports Health. 2010;2(4):279–283. Available at: http://www.ncbi. nlm.nih.gov/pmc/articles/PMC3445088/.

Gregory JE, Proske U. The responses of Golgi tendon organs to stimulation of different combinations of motor units. The Journal of Physiology. 1979;295:251-262. https://www.ncbi.nlm.nih.gov/pmc/articles/ PMC1279043/

Miller KC, Stone MS, Huxel KC, Edwards JE. Exercise-Associated Muscle Cramps: Causes, Treatment, and Prevention. Sports Health. 2010;2(4):279-283. doi:10.1177/1941738109357299. https://www.ncbi. nlm.nih.gov/pmc/articles/PMC3445088/

Behringer M, Moser M, McCourt M, Montag J, Mester J. A Promising Approach to Effectively Reduce Cramp Susceptibility in Human Muscles:

A Randomized, Controlled Clinical Trial. Hayashi N, ed. PLoS ONE. 2014;9(4):e94910. doi:10.1371/journal.pone.0094910. https://www.ncbi.nlm.nih.gov/pmc/articles/PMC3984281/

Sharkey, B.J. (1979) Physiology of Fitness: Prescribing Exercise for Fitness Weight Control and Health, Human Kinetics Publishers

Sharpening the Warrior's Edge: The Psychology & Science of Training (1995) by Bruce K Siddle, ISBN-10: 0964920506 ISBN-13: 978-0964920507

ABOUT THE AUTHOR

Photo: A. dEntremont

Rich Borgatti lives in Massachusetts with his wife, two boys and dog Torch. He owns and operates Mountain Strength Fitness in Winchester, Massachusetts. Rich is an early adopter of CrossFit and Obstacle Course Racing. He has been referred to as "One of the first OCR coaches in the world". He can often be found running in the Middlesex Fells Reservation near his gym.

Early on Rich combined his knowledge of Cross-Country Running, CrossFit, MovNat, Free Running and Track and Field to form the basis of his Obstacle Course Race Training programs. Some of the first workshops and seminars ever offered on the subject. He has gone on to earn multiple certifications in the world of endurance, strength and conditioning and Obstacle Course Racing.

Rich has been interviewed for podcasts, by Men's Health Magazine and in the CrossFit Journal on training athletes for OCRs. He has worked with hundreds of OCR athletes over the past decade in his gym, at seminars and through leading Spartan World Tour fitness events. In 2019 he was named one of the top 10 OCR coaches in America by Spartan Races. His interview was published in the first ever Spartan Magazine in December 2020. He has worked with brand new racers to elite podium winning athletes.

To work with Rich Borgatti
or media inquiries contact him at Rich@mountainstrength.com

http://www.richborgatti.com

http://www.mountainstrength.com

http://www.epicracetraining.com

Photo: J.Galvez